CW00552142

KEN BARRINGTON

by

Jerry Lodge

Published by the Association of Cricket Statisticians and Historians, West Bridgford, Nottingham
2001
Typeset by Limlow Books
Printed by Tranters, Derby
ISBN: 1 902171 49 7

Barrington with John Edrich after their stand
for England v New Zealand at Headingley in 1965

ACKNOWLEDGEMENTS

Brian Heald, Philip Bailey and Stephen Eley.

BIBLIOGRAPHY

Running into Hundreds by K. F. Barrington
Playing it Straight by K. F. Barrington
Cricket Facts & Feats by Bill Frindall
The Long Run by Alfred Gover
England Expects by Mark Peel
Ken Barrington - A Tribute by Brian Scovell

Surrey C.C.C. Year Books
Wisden Cricketers' Almanacks

Ken Barrington

Kenneth Frank Barrington was born on 24th November 1930 in Reading, the eldest son of a private soldier based in barracks in the town. He left school at the age of 14 to take up an apprenticeship as a motor mechanic, but a year later was offered a job as a groundboy at Reading C.C. which he gratefully accepted. He acted as an assistant to the Groundsman, Charlie Brockway, a Minor Counties player with Dorset and Berkshire. In those days he was primarily a bowler and was recommended to Surrey. On 27th May, 1947, he was invited to play for Surrey Colts at Hook and Southborough, Bernard Constable was also in the team; he took 5 wickets for 43 and scored 4 not out. In 1948 he joined the Surrey groundstaff and during the season had a game with Surrey 2nd XI against Norfolk when Peter May was in the same team.

Barrington was called up for National Service in 1949 where he served with the Wiltshire Regiment in Germany. At the time he was called up Barrington was 5ft 4in in height but by the time he was demobilised he had grown to 5ft 8in. His progress at Surrey was slow and he was fortunate to be retained on the staff but under the fatherly eye of Andy Sandham his batting steadily improved. His first match for Surrey 1st XI was in 1953 but he had a poor season despite scoring 81 against Worcestershire. His form improved in 1954 averaging over 40 with the bat in the season and sharing in a large stand of 198 with J.C.Laker for the eighth wicket against Gloucestershire. He made his Test debut in 1955 against South Africa and was dismissed for nought in his first innings. He was retained for the next match at Lord's but then dropped and did not play international cricket again until 1959. During the late 1950s Surrey dropped him on occasions and in 1958 he made a serious analysis of his batting technique to eliminate errors, which caused him to be often caught in the leg trap. With great help from his colleagues, he decided to get his head down and graft, which eliminated some of his more attractive strokes but had a major improvement in his run acquisition. In 1959, after scoring two centuries in one match against Warwickshire at Edgbaston, he won back his place in the England team against India and joining Peter May at the crease, he scored an excellent 80. On the 1959/60 tour to the West Indies, he scored his first Test century in a series won by England.

He was named as one of the "Five Cricketers of the Year" in *Wisden* in 1960. Quoted in this article describing his early years at Surrey - "For a time Barrington remained static as a batsman. Indeed, after all his promise he had two comparatively lean years in 1956 and 1958, but in 1957 his runs numbered 1642 and he hit six centuries, yet one felt that the best of him had not been seen. It should be borne in mind that during these formative years for Barrington, Surrey were winning the Championship regularly on pitches that encouraged the bowlers. Under Surridge and May, the batsmen were expected to make their runs in reasonable time and many people were of the opinion that Barrington did not show the enterprise that his ability warranted. Barrington, on the other hand, considers that his first five or six years in the Surrey team provided the sound education he needed to perfect his defence, as well as the experience required to get to the top of the cricketing world. He admits he also learnt much from being able to watch great players, particularly Peter May." Continuing the article observed "Built on solid lines with a mop of dark hair, Barrington has always possessed a powerful square cut and brilliant cover drives. Nowadays he is equipped with a wide range of strokes and when he is master of the situation he provides plenty of entertainment for the onlookers. The straight uplift of his bat is a model for anyone to copy."

With the visit of the Australians in 1961, Barrington made changes to his stance to counter the left arm fast bowling of Alan Davidson. For all his keenness in the field and the pride he felt from wicket taking, batting was always his main priority and the focus of his energy and concentration. Apart from his smartly groomed appearance, his gear would be in perfect condition. His bats, normally a light 2lb 3oz size, were carefully chosen, clearly marked and lovingly tended. Always a stickler for practice he preferred to have a net or at least hold a bat in his hand before the start of play each morning. More than most, he was a nervous starter because he placed such high stakes on the eventual outcome and his friends used to play on them in County matches. In his autobiography, Alf Gover, the Surrey fast bowler and coach comments "County cricket during most of Ken's career was played on pitches of variable bounce, so he collected runs, being content to push the straight ball and the short of a length delivery for singles. But if the ball was off line or length he gave it the necessary treatment. On overseas pitches, when he could judge the height of bounce off the pitch, he was a different player."

The Test Match career of Barrington showed that his performances overseas were better than those in England.

	M	Inn	NO	Runs	HS	Avge	100	50	Ct	Runs	Wkts	Avge
Home	46	73	7	3347	256	50.71	6	21	34	336	9	37.33
Overseas	36	58	8	3459	172	69.18	14	14	24	964	20	48.20
TOTAL	82	131	15	6806	256	58.67	20	35	58	1300	29	44.82

His career average against Australia was 63.97 from 23 matches and over 75 against India from 14 matches. Barrington achieved a unique feat when he exceeded 50 in each of ten first-class innings he played at the Adelaide Oval for England and the MCC. His scores were 104*, 52, 52*, 63 and 132* on the 1962/63 tour, and 69, 51, 63, 60 and 102 in 1965/66. This gave him an average of 93.50 on this ground which was bettered at Melbourne with 94.00. In England his best ground average was 77.63 at Old Trafford where he scored four centuries and seven 50s during fifteen matches on the ground. Whenever the early batsmen had failed to deliver the goods, Ken would invariably s' ɔ the rot. He never played any 'fancy' strokes, his approach to the bowling being, 'You will have to g me out, you won't get any help from me.' The Australians often said that, if England were in crises, you could almost see the Union Jack behind Barrington as he walked out to the wicket, giving the impression that this nonsense must stop. I know his fellow players appreciated his professional approach to the game.

During his career, Barrington was involved in 142 century partnerships, twenty of these with J.H.Edrich sixteen with M.J.Stewart and ten with P.B.H.May. Away from Surrey, the most partnerships over 100 were scored with M.C.Cowdrey (7). He was awarded a benefit in 1964, which raised £10,702.

In 1966 he missed several games as he was on the brink of a nervous breakdown. Controversy was never far away from Barrington. There was a long running saga with C.C.Griffith as Barrington believed that Griffith "threw" his faster delivery. This reached its zenith in 1966 and eventually led to Barrington having a physical and mental breakdown. When he went to the West Indies in 1967/68 he was taunted consistently by the crowds. However Barrington "came good" scoring 143 in the First Test at Port-of-Spain and was part of the triumphant England team. In his benefit match against Yorkshire, Trueman caught him and Barrington walked when Trueman confirmed that he had taken a clean catch. Later a photographer showed Barrington a picture of the dismissal, which appeared to cast doubt on Trueman's claim of a fair catch. A furious Barrington confronted Trueman but the matter was never resolved owing to lack of conclusive evidence either way. In South Africa, further controversy followed when he "walked" after being given not out by the umpire for a catch behind, an obvious point being made to the South Africans when one of their team had refused to walk on an earlier occasion, a straightforward catch having been taken for which the England players had not immediately appealed.

During his career, the one-day game was only in its infancy. The Gillette Cup started in 1963 and Barrington played in only 14 matches up to 1968 finishing on the winning side eight times. His batting average was 33.25 with 3 fifties, his highest score being 70. Limited Over International cricket did not start until 1970/71.

At the end of the 1968 English Season, Barrington undertook two small tours overseas. Firstly he went to Israel with the Bournemouth 5705 Club (the Jewish Year the Club was formed) and was installed as President of the Israel Cricket Supporters Club. He then went on to Melbourne to join Colin Milburn in a Double Wicket Tournament and, after winning their first match against Kanhai and Griffith, he was taken ill and suffered a minor heart attack. On doctor's advice he retired from first-class cricket in January 1969 at the age of 38. Although he was advised, subsequently, that he could play first-class cricket again if he wished, he gave way, quite contentedly, to discretion. Within two or three years he and his wife Ann were running a successful garage business in Bookham and Leatherhead, based on straight dealing, conviviality and a famous name. There was little Ken didn't know about cars, having been apprenticed as a motor mechanic before joining Surrey.

His son (Guy Kenneth) was born on 16th November 1969, Ken and Ann having been married since 1954.

After his retirement, he wrote on cricket for newspapers and in 1975 managed a tour to South Africa for Derrick Robins. In the same year he was appointed as a Test selector. He managed the England Tour to India, Sri Lanka and Australia in 1976/77 when the captain was Tony Greig and the following year managed the team to Pakistan and New Zealand with Mike Brearley as captain. It was his ambition that a permanent England manager should be appointed, but this did not come about until after his death.

He was Assistant Manager on three tours, first to Doug Insole on the 1978/79 tour to Australia which was captained by Mike Brearley, to Alec Bedser on the 1979/80 tour to Australia again captained by Brearley and, finally, to Alan Smith on the 1980/81 tour to the West Indies when Ian Botham was the captain. It was on this tour that Barrington suffered a fatal heart attack on 14th March 1981 during a Test match in Barbados whilst in the midst of a stressful period involving problems with the Guyanese Government who refused to let Robin Jackman participate because of his South African connections. The team was having a lean time and he put in a great deal of hard work to effect improvements. Alec Bedser, who was in the West Indies at the time told Alf Gover that Ken spent up to three hours in the hot sun bowling in the nets at the batsmen in an effort to show them how to tackle the West Indies attack.

Surrey, through its Youth Trust, decided that a suitable way of commemorating Barrington would be to build a Cricket Centre with indoor nets and other sporting facilities, which would provide opportunities for youngsters in the community - many from deprived areas - to learn the game of cricket and develop their characters. After considerable problems and a "Save the Oval" appeal, the Centre was opened by Her Majesty The Queen on 31st July 1991 when both Ann and Guy were presented to the royal party. As Mark Peel so eloquently states in his biography of Ken Barrington "the Barrington legacy lives on, a fount of inspiration to future generations who attempt to cross the great divide between poverty and affluence".

With his Test record of 6,800 runs, Ken's name has already become a legend in the history of Surrey and England cricket.

1953

His first appearances in first-class cricket were during the glory years of Surrey in the second year of their seven-year reign as County Champions. After two matches in May in non-Championship matches, he played throughout July but made only one score over fifty, which was against Worcestershire.

		Own Team Total	O	M	R	W		Opp Total	Ct
1. Surrey v MCC, Lord's, May 6, 7, 8 (MCC won by 107 runs)									
st T.G.Evans									
b A.S.M.Oakman	8	210						150	
c T.C.Dodds									
b A.S.M.Oakman	17	166						333-9d	
2. Surrey v Australians, Kennington Oval, May 9, 11 (Australians won by innings and 76 runs)									
c R.Benaud b R.G.Archer	10	58						256	1
c G.B.Hole b R.G.Archer	4	122							
3. Surrey v Sussex, Guildford, July 1, 2, 3 (Sussex won by seven wickets)									
lbw b D.J.Wood	4	145						253	
c D.V.Smith b A.E.James	12	213						106-3	
4. Surrey v Yorkshire, Kennington Oval, July 4, 6, 7 (Surrey won by ten wickets)									
b F.S.Trueman	24	292						137	
did not bat	-	21-0						172	
5. Surrey v Warwickshire, Edgbaston, July 8, 9, 10 (Warwickshire won by 140 runs)									
b J.D.Bannister	41	151						257	
c H.E.Dollery b C.W.C.Grove	8	99						133	
6. Surrey v Kent, Blackheath, July 11, 13, 14 (Match drawn)									
not out	15	302-5d						63	
								323	
7. Surrey v Worcestershire, Kennington Oval, July 15, 16, 17 (Surrey won by innings and 190 runs)									
c H.Yarnold									
b L.N.Devereux	81	371-6d						82	
								99	
8. Surrey v Leicestershire, Kennington Oval, July 18, 20, 21 (Surrey won by nine wickets)									
b J.E.Walsh	9	222						107	1
did not bat	-	63-1						177	
9. Surrey v Gloucestershire, Bristol, July 25, 27, 28 (Gloucestershire won by 97 runs)									
b C.J.Scott	0	213						269	1
b D.A.Allen	4	111						152-5d	1

SEASON'S AVERAGES

Batting and Fielding	M	I	NO	Runs	HS	Ave	100	50	Ct
Championship	7	10	1	198	81	22.00	-	1	3
Other Surrey matches	2	4	0	39	17	9.75	-	-	1
Season	9	14	1	237	81	18.23	-	1	4

1954

His six-year apprenticeship in company with some of the finest craftsmen in the business, including Laker, Lock, Surridge and Andy Sandham, the Surrey coach, was over and he was ready to go out and earn a living on his own merit. Two centuries in 16 Championship matches and one against the touring Pakistan team contributed to a season's average of 40. At the Oval, he shared in an eighth wicket partnership of 198 with J.C.Laker, who made his maiden first-class century, against Gloucestershire, which set up a victory by 145 runs.

		Own Team Total	O	M	R	W		Opp Total	Ct
10. Surrey v Leicestershire, Kennington Oval, May 12, 13, 14 (Match drawn)									
b V.E.Jackson	24	372						164	1
								128-7	

11. Surrey v Sussex, Hove, May 15, 17, 18 (Surrey won by one wicket)
lbw b R.G.Marlar   4   400-9d   -   -   -   -   369-9d
b A.S.M.Oakman   54   240-9   7   1   45   1   G.Cox c G.A.R.Lock   270-5d

12. Surrey v Somerset, Taunton, May 22, 24, 25 (Match drawn)
c H.W.Stephenson
    b M.F.Tremlett   4   366   220   1

13. Surrey v Cambridge University, Kennington Oval, June 19, 21 (Surrey won by an innings and 101 runs)
did not bat   -   380-4d   -   -   -   -   103   2
                              6   1   18   0   176   1

14. Surrey v Oxford University, Guildford, June 23, 24, 25 (Match drawn)
c C.C.P.Williams
    b D.C.P.R.Jowett   28   422-8d   161
                                            160-8   1

15. Surrey v Gloucestershire, Kennington Oval, July 14, 15, 16 (Surrey won by 145 runs)
not out   108   347-8d   326
c A.E.Wilson
    b F.P.McHugh   68   202-7d   78   1

16. Surrey v Pakistanis, Kennington Oval, July 17, 19, 20 (Match drawn)
c A.H.Kardar
    b M.E.Z.Ghazali 102   329-6   365-6d

17. Surrey v Essex, Colchester, July 21, 22, 23 (Match drawn)
b J.A.Bailey   2   229   264   1
not out   32   286-4d   133-5

18. Surrey v Kent, Blackheath, July 24, (26), 27 (Match drawn)
b D.V.P.Wright   1   387   202   2

19. Surrey v Essex, Kennington Oval, July 28, 29, 30 (Surrey won by ten wickets)
not out   89   233-9d   124
did not bat   -   4-0   109

20. Surrey v Nottinghamshire, Kennington Oval, July 31, August 2 (Surrey won by ten wickets)
b G.Goonesena   32   168   73
did not bat   -   21-0   113   1

21. Surrey v Northamptonshire, Kettering, August 4, 5 (Surrey won by one wicket)
lbw b V.Broderick   17   121   125   1
st L.Livingston
    b V.Broderick   22   139-9   133

22. Surrey v Middlesex, Kennington Oval, August 7, 9, 10 (Match drawn)
c W.J.Edrich b F.J.Titmus   31   193-5d   51

23. Surrey v Leicestershire, Leicester, August 11, 12, 13 (Surrey won by six wickets)
b J.S.Savage   24   185-4d   106
c M.J.K.Smith b J.S.Savage   0   40-4   117

24. Surrey v Gloucestershire, Cheltenham, August 14, 16, 17 (Surrey won by 156 runs)
lbw b F.P.McHugh   3   143   153-8d
b F.P.McHugh   103   278   112

25. Surrey v Worcestershire, Worcester, August 18, 19 (Surrey won by ten wickets)
b J.R.Ashman   22   279   184
did not bat   -   7-0   99

26. Surrey v Middlesex, Lord's, August 21, 23 (Surrey won by an innings and 19 runs)
run out   9   206-8d   70   2
                                           117

27. Surrey v Worcestershire, Kennington Oval, August 25, 26 (Surrey won by an innings and 27 runs)
not out   10   92-3d   25   2
                                           40

28. Surrey v Lancashire, Kennington Oval, August 28, 30, 31 (Surrey won by 93 runs)
c G.A.Edrich b J.B.Statham 43   128   160
c T.Greenhough
    b M.J.Hilton   13   213   88

SEASON'S AVERAGES

Batting and Fielding	M	I	NO	Runs	HS	Ave	100	50	Ct
Championship	16	23	4	715	108*	37.63	2	3	12
Other Surrey matches	3	2	0	130	102	65.00	1	-	4
Season	19	25	4	845	108*	40.23	3	3	16
Career	28	39	5	1082	108*	31.82	3	4	20

Bowling	O	M	R	W	BB	Ave	5i
Championship	13	2	63	1	1-45	63.00	-

1955

Playing for MCC against the South Africans, Barrington was dismissed for 3 and 27, being lbw to Trevor Goddard both times. Goddard bowled left arm accurate over the wicket seamers and it was this defect in his game that persuaded Barrington to change to a more open two-eyed stance. Scoring centuries in consecutive matches saw Barrington being awarded his county cap and a week later being selected for his first Test match. Like many a great batsman before him, he failed to "trouble the scorers" on his debut. He was retained for the Second Test at Lord's, but then lost his place and it was to be four years before he played for England again. However, Barrington made his full contribution to Surrey in retaining the County Championship. Although at this stage of his career Barrington had not done much bowling, he was asked to bowl in the Festival game at Torquay in September and took more than five wickets in an innings for the first time.

	Own Team Total	O	M	R	W	Opp Total	Ct
29. Surrey v Cambridge University, Fenner's, April 30, May 2, 3 (Surrey won by an innings and 70 runs)							
c D.J.Smith b S.Singh	66 328	-	-	-	-	82	
		7	0	31	0	176	
30. Surrey v MCC, Lord's, May 4, 5, 6 (Surrey won by seven wickets)							
b J.D.Bannister	14 159					129	1
not out	15 55-3					83	
31. Surrey v Gloucestershire, Kennington Oval, May 7, 9, 10 (Surrey won by eight wickets)							
c G.M.Emmett							
b J.B.Mortimore	46 232					126	
did not bat	- 33-2					137	
32. Surrey v Somerset, Kennington Oval, May 14, 16 (Surrey won by an innings and 4 runs)							
b J.W.J.McMahon	64 224					99	
						121	1
33. Surrey v Essex, Ilford, May 18, 19, 20 (Surrey won by five wickets)							
b D.J.Insole	39 179					126	
lbw b W.T.Greensmith	23 150-5					202	
34. MCC v South Africans, Lord's, May 21, 23, 24 (South Africans won by 93 runs)							
lbw b T.L.Goddard	3 87					185-9d	
lbw b T.L.Goddard	27 189					184	
35. Surrey v Lancashire, Kennington Oval, May 25, 26, 27 (Surrey won by an innings and 143 runs)							
not out	135 345-3d					94	
						108	
36. Surrey v Nottinghamshire, Trent Bridge, May 28, 30, 31 (Surrey won by eight wickets)							
c J.Hardstaff b P.F.Harvey	126 368-6d	-	-	-	-	353	
did not bat	- 188-2	4	0	22	0	202-7d	
37. Surrey v Glamorgan, Kennington Oval, June 1, 2, 3 (Surrey won by eight wickets)							
b W.Wooller	31 239					56	
did not bat	- 105-2					287	
38. Surrey v Yorkshire, Kennington Oval, June 4, 6, 7 (Surrey won by 41 runs)							
c D.B.Close R.Appleyard	1 85					131	
b J.H.Wardle	11 261-7d					174	2
39. ENGLAND v SOUTH AFRICA, Trent Bridge, June 9, 10, 11, 13 (England won by an innings and 5 runs)							
c J.H.B.Waite b E.R.H.Fuller	0 334					181	
						148	

40. Surrey v Cambridge University, Kennington Oval, June 15, 16, 17 (Surrey won by an innings and 23 runs)
    b D.J.Smith   9   337   112   1
                                                      202   1

41. Surrey v Yorkshire, Headingley, June 18, 20, 21 (Yorkshire won by six wickets)
    c J.V.Wilson b R.Appleyard 5   268   166
    b F.S.Trueman   0   75   178-4

42. ENGLAND v SOUTH AFRICA, Lord's, June 23, 24, 25, 27 (England won by 71 runs)
    b P.S.Heine   34   133   304
    c R.A.McLean
        b H.J.Tayfield   18   353   111

43. Surrey v Worcestershire, Kennington Oval, June 29, 30 (Surrey won by ten wickets)
    c D.W.Richardson
        b R.T.D.Perks 32   148-5d   77
    did not bat   -   85-0   153

44. Surrey v Kent, Blackheath, July 2, 4 (Surrey won by an innings and 28 runs)
    not out   5   340-5d   107
                                                  205

45. Surrey v Leicestershire, Kennington Oval, July 6, 7, 8 (Surrey won by five wickets)
    not out   27   319-5d   314-9d   1
    not out   28   161-5   165

46. Surrey v Kent, Kennington Oval, July 9, 11, 12 (Kent won by 13 runs)
    c R.C.Wilson b J.M.Allan 27   146   181
    lbw b J.M.Allan   72   138   116

47. Players v Gentlemen, Lord's, July 13, 14, 15 (Players won by 20 runs)
    c J.P.Fellows-Smith
        b J.J.Warr 3   316   336-8d   2
    st B.A.Barnett
        b G.Goonesena 0   220   180   1

48. Surrey v South Africans, Kennington Oval, July 16, 18, 19 (South Africans won by 82 runs)
    lbw b H.J.Tayfield   5   140   244
    c P.L.Winslow
        b H.J.Tayfield 34   192   170

49. Surrey v Glamorgan, Swansea, July 20, 21 (Surrey won by nine wickets)
    b A.J.Watkins   59   294   171
    did not bat   -   48-1   170

50. Surrey v Worcestershire, Worcester, July 23, 25, 26 (Surrey won by eight wickets)
    lbw b M.J.Horton   18   394-8d   158
    not out   8   35-2   270

51. Surrey v Warwickshire, Coventry, July 27, 28, 29 (Warwickshire won by 131 runs)
    run out   49   154   210
    b J.D.Bannister   34   175   250

52. Surrey v Nottinghamshire, Kennington Oval, July 30, August 1, 2 (Surrey won by an innings and 3 runs)
    b F.W.Stocks   43   295   252
                                                    40

53. Surrey v Lancashire, Old Trafford, August 3, 4, 5 (Surrey won by seven wickets)
    c J.Jordan b R.Tattersall 54   220   248   2
    not out   38   155-3   125

54. Surrey v Middlesex, Kennington Oval, August 6, 8, 9 (Surrey won by 39 runs)
    c L.H.Compton b F.J.Titmus 73 171   203
    c G.P.S.Delisle b J.A.Young 2   193   122

55. Surrey v Somerset, Weston-super-Mare, August 10, 11 (Surrey won by an innings and 100 runs)
    c M.F.Tremlett
        b J.W.J.McMahon 1   227   36
                                                   91

56. Surrey v Gloucestershire, Cheltenham, August 13, 15 (Surrey won by 43 runs)
    c C.A.Milton
        b G.E.E.Lambert 12   180   135-9d   1
    c J.F.Crapp b J.B.Mortimore 11 77   79

57. Surrey v Northamptonshire, Northampton, August 17, 18, 19 (Northamptonshire won by six wickets)
    c R.Subba Row c G.E.Tribe 1   215   - - - -   186
    b V.Broderick   15   173   2.5 0 20 0   205-4

58. Surrey v Middlesex, Lord's, August 20, 22, 23 (Surrey won by nine wickets)

b A.E.Moss	51	282						198	1
did not bat	-	32-1						115	1

59. Surrey v Sussex, Kennington Oval, August 24, 25, 26 (Surrey won by an innings and 8 runs)

c D.V.Smith b J.M.Parks	39	343-9d						245	
								90	

60. Surrey v Hampshire, Bournemouth, August 27, 29, 30 (Hampshire won by 129 runs)

b D.Shackleton	19	245	368-7d
c M.D.Burden b J.R.Gray	12	174	180-7d

61. Surrey v Derbyshire, Kennington Oval, August 31, September 1 (Surrey won by eight wickets)

c G.O.Dawkes b C.Gladwin	1	101	103	
c D.B.Carr b D.Hall	50	133-2	130	1

62. South v North, Torquay, September 3, 5, 6 (South won by 109 runs)

c K.V.Andrew b R.Tattersall	25	431	5	0	42	1	K.V.Andrew c F.J.Titmus	435-9d	2
st K.V.Andrew b J.E.Walsh	52	335-9d	15.4	0	70	6	D.Brookes c and b	222	1
							M.J.Horton c F.J.Titmus		
							V.E.Jackson lbw		
							J.E.Walsh c R.E.Marshall		
							K.V.Andrew b		
							C.Gladwin c W.E.Jones		

63. Surrey v The Rest, Kennington Oval, September 10, 12, 13, 14 (The Rest won by two wickets)

c J.V.Wilson b T.E.Bailey	13	165	299	1
b F.S.Trueman	0	297	164-8	1

SEASON'S AVERAGES

Batting and Fielding	M	I	NO	Runs	HS	Ave	100	50	Ct
Test matches	2	3	0	52	34	17.33	-	-	-
Players v Gentlemen	1	2	0	3	2	1.50	-	1	3
Championship	25	38	6	1262	135*	39.43	2	7	10
Other Surrey matches	5	8	1	156	66	22.28	-	1	5
Other matches	2	4	0	107	52	26.75	-	1	3
Season	35	55	7	1580	135*	32.91	2	9	21
Career	63	94	12	2662	135*	32.46	5	13	41

Bowling	O	M	R	W	BB	Ave	5i
Championship	6.5	0	42	0	-	-	-
Other Surrey matches	7	0	31	0	-	-	-
Other matches	20.4	0	112	7	6-70	16.00	1
Season	34.3	0	185	7	6-70	26.42	1
Career (6 ball)	47.3	2	248	8	6-70	31.00	1

1955/56 - MCC A in Pakistan

The MCC "A" Team to Pakistan was his first overseas tour that went sour after a childish prank upset a Pakistani umpire one evening in the hotel and this episode nearly led to an international incident. Despite averaging nearly 40 with the bat, it was an unhappy tour relieved only by the sense of humour of several of the players, notably Ken Barrington.

	Own Team Total		O	M	R	W		Opp Total	Ct
64. MCC A v Karachi C.A., Karachi, December 26, 27, 28 (Match drawn)									
not out	70	323-5d	4	1	15	0		204	
not out	4	156-3	6	0	23	0		182-4	
65. MCC A v Sind C.A., Hyderabad, January 6, (7), (8) (Match drawn)									
b Mohammad Munaf	66	336						2-2	
66. MCC A v Amir of Bahawalpur's XI, Bahawalpur, January 11, 12, 13 (MCC A won by an innings and 64 runs)									
run out	18	277	-	-	-	-		137	
			1	0	3	1	Ismail Ibrahim c G.A.R.Lock	76	

67. MCC A v Combined Universities, Lahore, January 16, 17, 18 (Match drawn)
```
   b Abdul Aziz        14   247    6.1  3   8  1  S.F.Rehman  b    256
   did not bat          -   60-2   10   4  20  0                  202-5d    1
```
68. MCC A v Pakistan, Lahore, January 20, 21, 22, 24, 25 (Match drawn)
```
   c Imtiaz Ahmed
     b Fazal Mahmood   10   204                                   363-9d
   st Imtiaz Ahmed
     b Alim-ud-Din     52   322-7
```
69. MCC A v East Pakistan, Chittagong, January 27, 28 (MCC A won by an innings and 101 runs)
```
   lbw b Yawar Saeed   65   259                                   103       1
                                                                  55
```
70. MCC A v Pakistan, Dacca, February 3, (4), 5, 7, 8 (Pakistan won by an innings and 10 runs)
```
   c Waqar Hassain
     b Khan Mohammad   43   172                                   287-9d
   lbw b Fazal Mahmood 11   105
```
71. MCC A v Punjab C.A., Lyallpur, February 17, 18 (MCC A won by an innings and 29 runs)
```
   lbw b Yawar Saeed   87   268                                   100
                                                                  139
```
72. MCC A v Pakistan, Peshawar, February 24, 25, 26, 27 (Pakistan won by seven wickets)
```
   lbw b A.H.Kardar    32   188                                   152
   b A.H.Kardar         0   111                                   149-3
```
73. MCC A v Pakistan Services, Sargodha, March 2, 3, 4 (Match drawn)
```
   c and b Shuja-ud-din Butt 35  297    -   -   -  -              307       1
   did not bat          -   36-3   1   1   0  0                   137-6d
```
74. MCC A v Combined Railways and Baluchistan, Muljan, March 5, 6, 7 (MCC A won by an innings and 23 runs)
```
   c Ghafoor Butt
     b Khalid Qureshi  41   280                                   126       2
                                                                  131
```
75. MCC A v Pakistan, Karachi, March 9, 10, 12, 13, 14 (MCC won by two wickets)
```
   b Fazal Mahmood     10   184                                   178       1
   c Imtiaz Ahmed
     b Mahmood Hussain 28   126-8d                                130
```

SEASON'S AVERAGES

Batting and Fielding	M	I	NO	Runs	HS	Ave	100	50	Ct
Other matches	12	17	2	586	87	39.06	-	5	6
Career	75	111	14	3248	135*	33.48	5	18	47

Bowling	O	M	R	W	BB	Ave	5i
Other matches	28.1	9	69	2	1-3	34.50	-
Career (6 ball)	75.4	11	317	10	6-70	31.70	1

1956

This was one of the worst seasons of Barrington's career. After being tried unsuccessfully as an opener he was dropped by Surrey before returning to bat at no. 5 in the batting order. Although he scored more than 1000 runs it was a poor season for Barrington averaging only 30, which was not helped by suffering from a broken toe at one stage.

	Own Team Total	O	M	R	W	Opp Total	Ct
76. Surrey v Cambridge University, Fenner's, April 28, 30 (Surrey won by an innings and 78 runs)
```
   c M.E.L.Melluish
     b D.J.Smith       59   284-8d                                86
                                                                  120       1
```
77. Surrey v MCC, Lord's, May 2, 3, 4 (MCC won by 55 runs)
```
   b C.T.Spencer       17   235                                   142
   c C.A.Milton b C.T.Spencer 18  118                             266
```

78. Surrey v Derbyshire, Kennington Oval, May 5, 7, 8 (Match drawn)
c A.Hamer b C.Gladwin	13	215						164		
b C.Gladwin	41	180						223-9	1

79. Surrey v Northamptonshire, Kennington Oval, May 9, 10, 11 (Northamptonshire won by seven wickets)
c G.E.Tribe b V.Broderick	15	240						309		1
b G.E.Tribe	3	204						136-3	

80. Surrey v Glamorgan, Cardiff, May 12, 14 (Surrey won by 168 runs)
st H.G.Davies b W.E.Jones	20	160						98		
c and b D.J.Shepherd	59	210						104	1

81. Surrey v Australians, Kennington Oval, May 16, 17, 18 (Surrey won by ten wickets)
c K.R.Miller b I.W.Johnson	4	347						259		
did not bat	-	20-0						107	

82. Surrey v Nottinghamshire, Trent Bridge, May 19, 21, 22 (Nottinghamshire won by 187 runs)
c A.K.Walker b K.Smales	0	117						220		
b K.Smales	8	128						212	

83. Surrey v Leicestershire, Leicester, May 23, 24, 25 (Surrey won by 143 runs)
c J.Firth b C.H.Palmer	24	238						211		
did not bat	-	194-7d						78	

84. Surrey v Hampshire, Portsmouth, June 9, 11, 12 (Hampshire won by 28 runs)
c J.R.Gray b M.D.Burden	1	126						191		
b R.E.Marshall	21	108						71	

85. MCC v Cambridge University, Lord's, June 13, 14, 15 (Cambridge University won by nine wickets)
lbw b D.J.Smith	11	126						303		
not out	62	199						25-1	

86. Surrey v Oxford University, Kennington Oval, June 20, 21, 22 (Surrey won by 54 runs)
c A.C.Walton b J.M.Allan	0	243	-	-	-	-		267-9d		
not out	23	237-2d	11	1	38	2	A.P.Walshe b	159	
							S.V.M.Clube c M.J.Stewart		

87. Surrey v Hampshire, Guildford, June 23, 25, 26 (Surrey won by 37 runs)
c H.M.Barnard										
b D.Shackleton	7	173	-	-	-	-		185		1
c A.W.H.Rayment										
b V.H.D.Cannings	103	250-4d	5	0	22	0		201		1

88. Surrey v Cambridge University, Guildford, June 27, 28, 29 (Match drawn)
not out	13	300-1d						294-8d		
not out	25	103-1	1	0	1	0		236-6d	

89. Surrey v Kent, Kennington Oval, June 30, July 2 (Surrey won by eight wickets)
c F.Ridgway b J.C.T.Page	2	226						148		1
not out	6	21-2						98		1

90. Surrey v Northamptonshire, Northampton, July 4, 5, 6 (Northamptonshire won by seven wickets)
not out	109	273-6d	-	-	-	-		296-5d		
b J.S.Manning	40	165	0.3	0	5	0		144-3	

91. Surrey v Kent, Blackheath, July 7, 9, 10 (Surrey won by an innings and 173 runs)
c F.Ridgway										
b D.V.P.Wright	32	404-4d						101		1
								130		1

92. Surrey v Gloucestershire, Kennington Oval, July 11, 12, 13 (Match drawn)
c C.A.Milton										
b J.B.Mortimore	7	361-5d	12	2	45	0		303		
not out	21	153-2d							

93. Surrey v Yorkshire, Bramall Lane, July 21, 23, 24 (Surrey won by 14 runs)
b P.N.Broughton	34	128						189		
c J.G.Binks b J.H.Wardle	35	157						82	

94. Surrey v Sussex, Hastings, July 25, 26, 27 (Surrey won by 62 runs)
b N.I.Thomson	95	313-8d						245		
lbw b R.G.Marlar	18	205-9d						211		1

95. Surrey v Essex, Kennington Oval, July 28, 30, 31 (Surrey won by 109 runs)
b J.A.Bailey	0	174						150		2
c and b W.T.Greensmith	58	231						146	

96. Surrey v Australians, Kennington Oval, August (1), 2, 3 (Match drawn)
lbw b K.R.Miller	15	181-9d						143		
								47-3	

13

97. Surrey v Nottinghamshire, Kennington Oval, August 4, (6), 7 (Match drawn)
c A.K.Walker b A.Jepson   0   87   244-9d
not out   63   107-4

98. Surrey v Essex, Clacton-on-Sea, August 8, 9, 10 (Surrey won by five wickets)
c B.Taylor b J.A.Bailey   11   310-9d   193
lbw b R.Smith   4   61-5   176

99. Surrey v Middlesex, Kennington Oval, August 11, 13, 14 (Surrey won by seven wickets)
c D.C.S.Compton b J.J.Warr 47   176-9d   69   1
b W.J.Edrich   17   84-3   188

100. Surrey v Sussex, Kennington Oval, August 15, 16, 17 (Surrey won by seven wickets)
lbw b K.G.Suttle   19   196   175   1
c R.T.Webb b R.G.Marlar   2   104-3   124   1

101. Surrey v Middlesex, Lord's, August 18, 20, 21 (Surrey won by 71 runs)
c D.C.S.Compton
               b J.A.Young   15   113   63   2
c G.P.S.Delisle b J.A.Young 1   158-9d   137

102. Surrey v Derbyshire, Derby, August 22, 23, 24 (Match drawn)
lbw b D.Hall   0   197   210
not out   10   154-3d   85-4

103. Surrey v Warwickshire, Edgbaston, August 25, (27), 28 (Match drawn)
not out   22   181-3d   126
                                                        36-1

104. Surrey v Lancashire, Kennington Oval, August 29, (30), (31) (Match drawn)
c J.Jordan b M.J.Hilton   26   96   42-0

105. Surrey v Worcestershire, Worcester, September 1, 3, 4 (Match drawn)
c and b R.Berry   42   218   157
                                                        17-0

106. Surrey v The Rest, Kennington Oval, September 8, (10), 11 (The Rest won by 128 runs)
b F.S.Trueman   4   71   192   2
c T.W.Graveney
     b M.J.Hilton   21   72   79-3d

SEASON'S AVERAGES

Batting and Fielding	M	I	NO	Runs	HS	Ave	100	50	Ct
Championship	23	41	6	1051	109*	30.05	2	4	17
Other Surrey matches	7	11	3	199	59	24.87	-	1	3
Other matches	1	2	1	73	62*	73.00	-	1	-
Season	31	54	10	1323	109*	30.06	2	6	20
Career	106	165	24	4571	135*	32.41	7	24	67

Bowling	O	M	R	W	BB	Ave	5i
Championship	17.3	2	72	0	-	-	-
Other Surrey matches	12	1	39	2	2-38	19.50	-
Season	29.3	3	111	2	2-38	55.50	-
Career (6 ball)	101.1	14	428	12	6-70	35.66	1

1957

Barrington had a much better season in Surrey's Championship winning side scoring over 1600 runs at an average of nearly 40, including 103 against the full West Indies attack. Following the retirement of Surridge, he moved to fielding in the slips and took 64 catches in the season which with M.J.Stewart catching 77 and G.A.R.Lock 63 emphasised the high standard of close fielding during the Surrey winning run.

	Own Team Total	O	M	R	W		Opp Total	Ct
107. Surrey v Cambridge University, Fenner's, April 27, 29 (Surrey won by ten wickets)								
b C.S.Smith	16 240						140	1
did not bat	- 7-0						104	2

108. Surrey v MCC, Lord's, May 1, 2, 3 (Surrey won by 238 runs)
    c B.Taylor b D.Bennett   5   318-8d   149   1
    c C.H.Palmer b R.G.Marlar   4   199-6d   130   2

109. Surrey v Combined Services, Kennington Oval, May 4, 6, 7 (Match drawn)
    c G.A.Atkinson
        b D.B.Pearson   7   234   -   -   -   -   222   1
    not out   110 256-1d   3   1   12   1   S.A.Leadbetter c P.J.Loader 128-4

110. Surrey v Glamorgan, Kennington Oval, May 11, 13 (Surrey won by an innings and 166 runs)
    c A.J.Watkins
        b J.E.MCConnon   52 259   62   2
                                                    31   1

111. Surrey v Worcestershire, Kennington Oval, May 18, 20 (Surrey won by eight wickets)
    c D.Kenyon b R.Berry   36 109   108   2
    not out   30   90-2   90   2

112. Surrey v Sussex, Kennington Oval, May 22, 23, 24 (Match drawn)
    b R.G.Marlar   11 320-7d   144
    b N.I.Thomson   5   136-5d   141-4

113. Surrey v Leicestershire, Leicester, May 25, 27 (Surrey won by 222 runs)
    c C.T.Spencer b J.S.Savage 26 196   122
    c C.H.Palmer b V.S.Munden 6   248-5d   100   2

114. Surrey v Northamptonshire, Kennington Oval, May 29, 30, 31 (Northamptonshire won by 72 runs)
    b F.H.Tyson   4 116   -   -   -   -   113   3
    c A.P.Arnold b G.E.Tribe 5 157   11   1   34   2   D.W.Barrick c A.V.Bedser 232   2
                                                           B.L.Reynolds c and b

115. Surrey v Essex, Kennington Oval, June 1, 3 (Surrey won by an innings and 87 runs)
    c K.C.Preston b I.M.King 44 346-9d   -   -   -   -   123
                                  8   2   18   1   G.W.Horrex
                                                    c D.G.W.Fletcher 136

116. Surrey v Northamptonshire, Northampton, June 5, 6, 7 (Surrey won by ten wickets)
    b H.R.A.Kelleher   10 311   213
    did not bat   -   14-0   111   1

117. Surrey v Nottinghamshire, Trent Bridge, June 8, 10, 11 (Surrey won by an innings and 119 runs)
    not out   10 303-4d   125
                                                        59   1

118. Surrey v West Indians, Kennington Oval, June 12, 13, 14 (Match drawn)
    c J.D.C.Goddard
        b S.Ramadhin   26 210   -   -   -   -   220
    run out   2 270-6d   4   1   20   0   178-8   1

119. Surrey v Lancashire, Old Trafford, June 15, 17, 18 (Surrey won by an innings and 51 runs)
    not out   51 352-5d   135
                                                166   1

120. Surrey v Gloucestershire, Kennington Oval, June 19, 20 (Surrey won by an innings and 149 runs)
    not out   124 321-3d   68
                                               104

121. Surrey v Oxford University, Guildford, June 22, 24, 25 (Surrey won by 138 runs)
    b R.L.Jowett   76 368-4d   -   -   -   -   221
    did not bat   - 162-2d   3   0   14   0   171   1

122. Surrey v Hampshire, Guildford, June 26, 27 (Surrey won by an innings and 73 runs)
    not out   40 247-4d   66
                                               108   1

123. Surrey v Yorkshire, Kennington Oval, June 29, July 1, 2 (Surrey won by an innings and 19 runs)
    c J.G.Binks b F.S.Trueman 53 365   172
                                               174

124. Surrey v Derbyshire, Derby, July 3, 4, 5 (Surrey won by eight wickets)
    c G.O.Dawkes b H.L.Jackson 1 160   146   2
    not out   27 140-2   153   2

125. Surrey v Kent, Kennington Oval, July 6, 8 (Surrey won by ten wickets)
    c R.C.Wilson b J.F.Pretlove 43 181   57   2
    did not bat   -   67-0   190   2

126. Surrey v Derbyshire, Kennington Oval, July 10, 11, 12 (Match drawn)
    b D.C.Morgan   4 264   79   3
    c G.O.Dawkes b H.L.Jackson 0 2-1   208   2

127. Surrey v Yorkshire, Bradford, July (13), 15, 16 (Match drawn)
c F.S.Trueman
      b R.Illingworth   2   196-7d   91   2
                                                 121-7

128. Surrey v Leicestershire, Kennington Oval, July 17, 18, 19 (Surrey won by ten wickets)
not out   59   157-3d   87   2
did not bat   -   12-0   78   2

129. Surrey v Kent, Blackheath, July 20, 22, 23 (Surrey won by 73 runs)
c J.F.Pretlove b A.Brown   18   163   76   1
b A.Brown   4   141-7d   155   1

130. Surrey v Gloucestershire, Bristol, July 27, 29, 30 (Gloucestershire won by 38 runs)
c J.B.Mortimore b D.R.Smith 1   263-9d   249
c C.A.Milton b C.Cook   56   191   243-8d

131. Surrey v West Indians, Kennington Oval, July 31, August 1, 2 (West Indians won by seven wickets)
c O.G.Smith b S.Ramadhin 24 210   -   -   -   -   140   1
not out   103 199-3d   3   0   11   0   270-3   1

132. Surrey v Nottinghamshire, Kennington Oval, August 3, 5, 6 (Surrey won by six wickets)
c A.Jepson b G.Goonesena 19 293   226
st G.Millman b M.Morgan 8 107-4   173   1

133. Surrey v Hampshire, Portsmouth, August 7, 8 (Surrey won by an innings and 35 runs)
b P.J.Sainsbury   52 386-6d   120   2
                                               231   1

134. Surrey v Middlesex, Kennington Oval, August 10, 12, (13) (Match drawn)
b J.J.Warr   1   100-7   114   1

135. Surrey v Somerset, Weston-super-Mare, August 14, 15, 16 (Surrey won by three wickets)
c H.W.Stephenson
      b B.A.Langford   6 286   250
c and b C.L.McCool   32 153-7   188

136. Surrey v Middlesex, Lord's, August 17, 19, 20 (Surrey won by 102 runs)
b R.J.Hurst   0 178   100   1
b J.J.Warr   6 207   183   1

137. Surrey v Warwickshire, Edgbaston, August 24, 26, 27 (Surrey won by ten wickets)
b A.Townsend   101 392   -   -   -   -   186   1
did not bat   -   13-0   4   1   18   0   218   1

138. Surrey v Essex, Clacton-on-Sea, August 28, 29, 30 (Essex won by two wickets)
not out   129 367-7d   234   2
c B.Taylor b K.C.Preston 16 119   256-8   1

139. Surrey v Warwickshire, Kennington Oval, August 31, September 2 (Surrey won by an innings and 70 runs)
lbw b R.G.Carter   0 251   95
                                             86

140. Surrey v Sussex, Hove, September 4, 5, 6 (Surrey won by seven wickets)
c D.V.Smith b R.V.Bell 10 174   147   1
not out   27   89-3   115

141. Surrey v The Rest, Scarborough, September 11, 12, 13 (Surrey won by six wickets)
c G.E.Tribe b T.E.Bailey 136 369-7d   210   1
b F.S.Trueman   4 82-4   239

SEASON'S AVERAGES

Batting and Fielding	M	I	NO	Runs	HS	Ave	100	50	Ct
Championship	28	41	9	1129	129*	35.28	3	6	52
Other Surrey matches	7	12	2	513	136	51.30	3	1	12
Season	35	53	11	1642	136	39.09	6	7	64
Career	141	218	35	6213	136	33.95	13	31	131

Bowling	O	M	R	W	BB	Ave	5i
Championship	23	4	70	3	1-12	23.33	-
Other Surrey matches	13	2	57	1	1-18	57.00	-
Season	36	6	127	4	1-12	31.75	-
Career (6 ball)	141.1	20	555	16	6-70	34.68	1

1958

After a winter spent coaching in South Africa, Barrington had a very poor season, scoring just over 1100 runs at an average of 31. This was the watershed year for him. Dropped by Surrey for the home match against Lancashire, he was run out for a duck on his return against Yorkshire. He spent the remaining weeks of the season endeavouring to correct the mistakes in his batting and decided that radical changes were required as he was being dismissed too often by in-swing and off-break bowlers and being caught on the leg side. He decided to take fewer risks and become a grafter. He was to become an "averages" man, a less exciting player to watch but a dependable anchor man in whatever side he played.

	Own	Team Total	O	M	R	W		Opp Total	Ct
142. Surrey v Cambridge University, Fenner's, April (26), 28, 29 (Match drawn)									
c C.D.White b A.Hurd	34	207	8.2	3	20	2	P.I.Pieris c and b	164	3
							C.B.Howland c and b		
			7	2	31	4	R.M.Prideaux c J.C.Laker	129-8	
							R.M.James c M.J.Stewart		
							P.I.Pieris lbw		
							C.B.Howland c M.J.Stewart		
143. Surrey v MCC, Lord's, May 3, 5, 6 (MCC won by an innings and 3 runs)									
c A.S.M.Oakman b A.E.Moss 2		116						401-4d	
c M.J.K.Smith b F.H.Tyson 10		282							
144. Surrey v New Zealanders, Kennington Oval, May 7, 8 (Surrey won by an innings and 163 runs)									
c B.Sutcliffe b A.M.Moir	18	288						74	
								51	1
145. Surrey v Gloucestershire, Kennington Oval, May 10, 12, 13 (Surrey won by nine wickets)									
c B.J.Meyer b D.R.Smith	0	336-7d	-	-	-	-		126	1
not out	8	50-1	9	2	20	1	T.W.Graveney b	257	2
146. Surrey v Warwickshire, Kennington Oval, May 17, 19, 20 (Surrey won by an innings and 80 runs)									
c R.G.Carter b K.Ibadulla	1	305-9d						162	
								63	1
147. Surrey v Leicestershire, Kennington Oval, May 21, 22, 23 (Surrey won by an innings and 5 runs)									
b C.T.Spencer	33	278	-	-	-	-		126	1
			6	1	9	0		147	2
148. Surrey v Nottinghamshire, Trent Bridge, May 24, 26, 27 (Surrey won by an innings and 43 runs)									
not out	7	334-4d						188	
								103	
149. Surrey v Lancashire, Old Trafford, May 28, 29, 30 (Surrey won by 177 runs)									
st A.Wilson b M.J.Hilton	74	314						193	1
c sub b K.Higgs	14	83-4d						27	1
150. Surrey v Essex, Kennington Oval, May 31, June 2, 3 (Match drawn)									
c D.J.Insole b K.C.Preston	29	308	4	1	9	1	T.E.Bailey c P.B.H.May	276	2
151. Surrey v Northamptonshire, Kennington Oval, June 4, 5, 6 (Match drawn)									
not out	62	378-5d	22	6	63	1	K.V.Andrew c and b	529-9	3
152. Surrey v Somerset, Taunton, June 7, 8, 9 (Somerset won by six wickets)									
c P.J.Eele b B.A.Langford	8	347-8d	15	2	49	0		349-6d	1
c J.G.Lomax b B.A.Langford 3		113	-	-	-	-		112-4	2
153. Surrey v Yorkshire, Bramall Lane, June 14, 16, 17 (Yorkshire won by 248 runs)									
run out	0	94	-	-	-	-		138	1
lbw b J.H.Wardle	34	119	5	0	16	0		323-7d	1
154. Surrey v Derbyshire, Chesterfield, June (21), 23, 24 (Match drawn)									
c D.B.Carr b C.Gladwin	3	59-4						216-9d	2
155. Surrey v Cambridge University, Guildford, June 25, 26, (27) (Match drawn)									
lbw b R.M.James	80	202						85	
not out	40	178-4							
156. Surrey v Hampshire, Guildford, June (28), 30, July 1 (Match drawn)									
b D.Shackleton	9	106						201-8d	1
did not bat	-	2-0							

157. Surrey v Oxford University, Kennington Oval, July (2), 3, 4 (Match drawn)
    not out   75   171   -   -   -   -   140   1
                                              15   5   28   1   L.D.Watts c R.A.E.Tindall   56-2

158. Surrey v Kent, Kennington Oval, July 5, 7, 8 (Surrey won by ten wickets)
    b A.Brown   37   278-8d -   -   -   -   143
    did not bat   -   60-0   5   1   28   0   191

159. Surrey v Glamorgan, Swansea, July 9, 10, 11 (Surrey won by five wickets)
    c A.J.Watkins
          b D.J.Shepherd   10   254   280-9d
    did not bat   -   173-5   143

160. Surrey v Glamorgan, Kennington Oval, July 16, 17, 18 (Match drawn)
    c J.S.Pressdee
          b D.J.Shepherd   17   203   -   -   -   -   92   2
                                              26   5   64   1   P.M.Walker c R.Swetman   256-6   1

161. Surrey v Yorkshire, Kennington Oval, July 19, 21 (Surrey won by an innings and 88 runs)
    c F.S.Trueman
          b R.Illingworth   4   274   70   1
                                                                                                     116   1

162. Surrey v Gloucestershire, Bristol, July 23, 24, 25 (Match drawn)
    c B.J.Meyer b D.R.Smith   18   262   -   -   -   -   149   2
                                               4   0   25   0   322-6

163. Surrey v Essex, Leyton, July 26, 28 (Essex won by an innings and 33 runs)
    b K.C.Preston   10   79   186   1
    c K.C.Preston
          b L.H.R.Ralph   13   74

164. Surrey v New Zealanders, Kennington Oval, July 30, 31 (Surrey won by an innings and 103 runs)
    b J.C.Alabaster   11   275   -   -   -   -   54   3
                                              14.4 3   27   4   N.S.Harford   c M.J.Stewart   118   1
                                                                J.T.Sparling c P.B.H.May
                                                                J.C.Alabaster c M.J.Stewart
                                                                J.A.Hayes   c M.J.Stewart

165. Surrey v Nottinghamshire, Kennington Oval, August 2, 4 (Surrey won by eight wickets)
    c C.J.Poole b J.Cotton   17   153   142   1
    did not bat   -   96-2   106   1

166. Surrey v Leicestershire, Leicester, August 6, 7, 8 (Match drawn)
    not out   101   404-8d -   -   -   -   173
                                               2   0   5   0   177-2

167. Surrey v Middlesex, Kennington Oval, August 9, 11 (Surrey won by seven wickets)
    lbw b A.E.Moss   14   168   122   1
    did not bat   -   88-3   131   1

168. Surrey v Middlesex, Lord's, August 16, 18, 19 (Surrey won by six wickets)
    c J.T.Murray b A.E.Moss   37   176   197
    not out   9   111-4   89   2

169. Surrey v Northamptonshire, Northampton, August 20, 21, 22 (Match drawn)
    did not bat   -   130-3d   119   2
                                                                                                     38-3

170. Surrey v Worcestershire, Worcester, August 23, 25, 26 (Surrey won by nine wickets)
    c D.W.Richardson
          b D.B.Pearson   28   270-9d -   -   -   -   82   1
    did not bat   -   51-1   1   0   1   0   235

171. Surrey v Somerset, Kennington Oval, August 27, (28), 29 (Match drawn)
    c P.J.Eele b B.A.Langford   13   313-9d   66   2

172. Surrey v Sussex, Hove, August 30, September 1 (Surrey won by 17 runs)
    c Nawab of Pataudi
          b D.L.Bates   4   83   85   2
    not out   30   89   70

173. Surrey v Worcestershire, Kennington Oval, September 3, (4), 5 (Worcestershire won by 117 runs)
    not out   0   110-2d   230   1
    c M.J.Horton b J.A.Flavell   9   57   54-5d 1

174. South v North, Torquay, September 6, 8, 9 (South won by 38 runs)
    c R.Illingworth
          b H.L.Jackson   46   256   11   3   49   0   227
    c K.V.Andrew b C.Gladwin   44   215   -   -   -   -   206

175. England XI v A Commonwealth XI, Torquay, September 10, 11, 12 (A Commonwealth XI won by two
wickets)

c G.St. A.Sobers			
b W.E.Alley	75	276	277-8d
c F.M.M.Worrell			
b P.B.Wight	56	311-6d	311-8 1

SEASON'S AVERAGES

Batting and Fielding	M	I	NO	Runs	HS	Ave	100	50	Ct
Championship	26	33	7	656	101*	25.23	1	2	45
Other Surrey matches	6	8	2	270	80	45.00	-	2	9
Other matches	2	4	0	221	75	55.25	-	2	1
Season	34	45	9	1147	101*	31.86	1	6	55
Career	175	263	44	7360	136	33.60	14	37	186

Bowling	O	M	R	W	BB	Ave	5i
Championship	99	18	289	4	1-9	72.25	-
Other Surrey matches	45	13	106	11	4-27	9.63	-
Other matches	11	3	49	0	-	-	-
Season	155	34	444	15	4-27	29.60	-
Career (6 ball)	296.1	54	999	31	6-70	32.22	1

1959

A century in both innings against Warwickshire at Edgbaston and another 100 against
Nottinghamshire at Trent Bridge meant that Barrington scored more than 800 runs by the end of May
and led to his recall to England colours. This time he was determined not to fail and scored four fifties
in the five match series against India. In the first match he joined his captain, P.B.H.May, at the
wicket and scored 56. A total of 2499 runs in the season at an average of over 54 saw him finish fourth
in the national batting averages. Surrey surrendered the Championship to Yorkshire, finishing third in
an exciting season.

		Own Team Total	O	M	R	W		Opp Total	Ct
176. Surrey v Cambridge University, Fenner's, April 25, 27, 28 (Match drawn)									
c A.Wheelhouse b D.Kirby	97	238-5d						152-7	
177. Surrey v MCC, Lord's, May 2, 4, 5 (MCC won by 165 runs)									
c and b B.A.Langford	25	146	3	0	13	0		283-6d	1
lbw b A.E.Moss	8	104	-	-	-	-		132	1
178. Surrey v Warwickshire, Edgbaston, May 9, 11, 12 (Warwickshire won by six wickets)									
c F.C.Gardner b K.Ibadulla	186	344-6d	9	2	21	0		346-6d	
not out	118	235-3d	-	-	-	-		234-4	
179. Surrey v Indians, Kennington Oval, May 13, 14, 15 (Match drawn)									
run out	85	253	2	1	2	0		249	
not out	59	151-2	4	0	22	1	P.R.Umrigar st R.Swetman	205-3d	
180. Surrey v Nottinghamshire, Trent Bridge, May 16, 18, 19 (Match drawn)									
c C.J.Poole b J.D.Springall	4	350-7d	11	1	36	0		329	
not out	113	251-2d	13	1	33	1	R.T.Simpson c A.V.Bedser	111-2	
181. Surrey v Glamorgan, Kennington Oval, May 20, 21, 22 (Match drawn)									
b F.Clarke	21	276-9d						191	2
did not bat	-	53-0							
182. Surrey v Somerset, Kennington Oval, May 23, 25, 26 (Surrey won by nine wickets)									
c H.W.Stephenson									
b K.E.Palmer	73	188	7	0	22	0		331-5d	1
not out	13	225-1	-	-	-	-		79	
183. Surrey v Kent, Kennington Oval, May 30, June 1, 2 (Match drawn)									
c J.F.Pretlove b J.C.T.Page	35	340-6d	-	-	-	-		242	
lbw b J.C.T.Page	40	183-3d	19	3	58	1	S.E.Leary c P.B.H.May	164-5	

184. ENGLAND v INDIA, Trent Bridge, June 4, 5, 6, 8 (England won by an innings and 59 runs)
b R.G.Nadkarni   56 422   206   1
  157

185. Surrey v Yorkshire, Kennington Oval, June 13, 15, 16 (Surrey won by 86 runs)
b R.K.Platt   81 277-9d   145 4
lbw b R.K.Platt   3 87   133

186. ENGLAND v INDIA, Lord's, June 18, 19, 20 (England won by eight wickets)
c sub b R.B.Desai   80 226   168
did not bat   - 108-2   165

187. Surrey v Cambridge University, Guildford, June 24, 25, 26 (Surrey won by ten wickets)
c H.C.Blofeld b A.Hurd   149 382-3d - - - -   165 1
did not bat   - 37-0   10 3 26 0   253 1

188. Surrey v Sussex, Guildford, June 27, 29, 30 (Surrey won by nine wickets)
c K.G.Suttle b A.E.James   25 218   153 2
not out   6 42-1   102 1

189. ENGLAND v INDIA, Headingley, July 2, 3, 4 (England won by an innings and 173 runs)
c N.S.Tamhane
    b R.G.Nadkarni   80 483   161
  149 1

190. Surrey v Glamorgan, Cardiff, July 8, 9, 10 (Surrey won by ten wickets)
c D.J.Evans b D.J.Ward   5 392   211 2
did not bat   - 4-0   184

191. Surrey v Kent, Blackheath, July 11, 13, 14 (Surrey won by ten wickets)
c T.G.Evans b A.Brown   16 391-9d - - - -   143 1
did not bat   - 17-0   6 2 16 0   261 3

192. Players v Gentlemen, Lord's, July 15, 16, 17 (Match drawn)
c D.B.Carr b D.M.Sayer   4 365 - - - -   194 1
did not bat   - 49-0   9 2 25 1 E.R.Dexter c and b   319-5d 3

193. Surrey v Yorkshire, Bradford, July 18, 20, 21 (Surrey won by 48 runs)
c J.G.Binks b R.K.Platt   3 153   91 2
c D.Wilson b F.S.Trueman   3 159   173

194. ENGLAND v INDIA, Old Trafford, July 23, 24, 25, 27, 28 (England won by 171 runs)
lbw b Surendranath   87 490   14 3 36 3 C.G.Borde c and b   208 1
                              R.G.Nadkarni b
                              R.B.Desai b
lbw b R.G.Nadkarni   46 265-8d 27 4 75 2 P.R.Umrigar c R.Illingworth 376 1
                              Surendranath c F.S.Trueman

195. Surrey v Indians, Kennington Oval, July 29, 30, 31 (Match drawn)
b S.P.Gupte   47 214 - - - -   154
not out   25 64-5   3 2 1 0   139 1

196. Surrey v Nottinghamshire, Kennington Oval, August 1, 3, 4 (Surrey won by 57 runs)
b J.D.Springall   4 261   121
c G.Millman b M.Morgan   51 176-3d 5 0 12 0   259 1

197. Surrey v Worcestershire, Worcester, August 5, 6, 7 (Worcestershire won by 135 runs)
c M.J.Horton b J.A.Flavell   99 272   9 0 36 0   328 1
c D.W.Richardson b D.Pratt   11 118 - - - -   197-4d

198. Surrey v Middlesex, Lord's, August 8, 10, 11 (Match drawn)
lbw b F.J.Titmus   166 346   331-9d
  53-1

199. Surrey v Lancashire, Kennington Oval, August 12, 13, 14 (Lancashire won by ten wickets)
c G.Clayton b C.Hilton   64 204-9d 9 1 22 0   315-9d 1
b C.Hilton   19 180 - - - -   70-0

200. Surrey v Hampshire, Portsmouth, August 15, 17, 18 (Match drawn)
c L.Harrison
    b V.H.D.Cannings   44 220-9d   341-4d 2
b V.H.D.Cannings   100 266-9   156

201. ENGLAND v INDIA, Kennington Oval, August 20, 21, 22, 24 (England won by an innings and 27 runs)
c sub b S.P.Gupte   8 361   6 0 24 0   140 1
     - - - -   194

202. Surrey v Gloucestershire, Gloucester, August 26, 27 (Surrey won by 89 runs)
c C.A.Milton b D.R.Smith   12 130   101 1
c C.A.Milton b C.Cook   49 131   71

203. Surrey v Middlesex, Kennington Oval, August 29, 30, September 1 (Match drawn)

lbw b F.J.Titmus	40	219	9	1	37	1	J.T.Murray c J.C.Laker	308
run out	7	129-9	-	-	-	-		175-9d 1

204. Surrey v Northamptonshire, Kennington Oval, September 2, 3, 4 (Northamptonshire won by four wickets)

lbw b F.H.Tyson	0	206	218	1
b J.S.Manning	87	214	203-6	

205. Players v Gentlemen, Scarborough, September 5, 7, 8 (Players won by ten wickets)

b T.E.Bailey	32	376	15	2	59	4	D.J.Insole c F.S.Trueman	293 1
							J.R.Burnet b	
							R.V.C.Robins b	
							G.W.Richardson c D.E.V.Padgett	
did not bat	-	16-0	6	2	10	1	J.Brown c H.J.Rhodes	115

206. T.N.Pearce's XI v Indians, Scarborough, September 9, 10, 11 (T.N.Pearce's XI won by five wickets)

b Surendranath	48	252	-	-	-	-		176 2
st P.G.Joshi b R.G.Nadkarni	32	235-5	4	.0	15	0		310 2

207. The Rest v Yorkshire, Kennington Oval, September 12, 14, 15 (Yorkshire won by 66 runs)

st J.G.Binks b R.Illingworth	15	384-8d	5	0	18	3	R.Illingworth c D.B.Carr	160
							F.S.Trueman	
							R.K.Platt b	
c J.B.Bolus b R.Illingworth	18	135	22	4	72	2	D.Wilson b	425
							J.R.Burnet b	

SEASON'S AVERAGES

Batting and Fielding	M	I	NO	Runs	HS	Ave	100	50	Ct
Test matches	5	6	0	357	87	59.50	-	4	5
Players v Gentlemen	2	2	0	36	32	18.00	-	-	5
Championship	18	32	4	1498	186	53.50	5	6	26
Other Surrey matches	5	8	2	495	149	82.50	1	3	5
Other matches	2	4	0	113	48	28.25	-	-	4
Season	32	52	6	2499	186	54.32	6	13	45
Career	207	315	50	9859	186	37.20	20	50	231

Bowling	O	M	R	W	BB	Ave	5i
Test matches	47	7	135	5	3-36	27.00	-
Players v Gentlemen	30	9	94	6	4-59	15.80	-
Championship	97	11	293	3	1-33	97.66	-
Other Surrey matches	22	6	64	1	1-22	64.00	-
Other matches	31	1	105	5	3-18	21.00	-
Season	227	34	691	20	4-59	34.55	-
Career (6 ball)	523.1	88	1690	51	6-70	33.13	1

1959/60 - Surrey in Rhodesia

A short two match tour undertaken by Surrey to Rhodesia saw Barrington score one century in the first match which was lost by two runs.

	Own Team Total	O	M	R	W		Opp Total	Ct
208. Surrey v Rhodesia, Police 'A' (Upper) Ground, Salisbury, October 10, 11, 12 (Rhodesia won by 2 runs)								
c P.N.F.Mansell								
b J.Partridge	111 297	-	-	-	-		246	
c C.A.R.Duckworth								
b P.N.F.Mansell	30 107	23	5	48	3	C.A.R.Duckworth c W.S.Surridge	160	
						D.Lewis c R.Swetman		
						R.Ullyett c R.Swetman		
209. Surrey v Rhodesia, Bulawayo, October 17, 18, 19 (Match drawn)								
c L.Koch b R.Ullyett	4 75	23	3	83	2	D.Lewis c A.V.Bedser	321	1
						C.A.R.Duckworth c E.A.Bedser		
c and b P.N.F.Mansell	20 380						53-3	2

SEASON'S AVERAGES

Batting and Fielding	M	I	NO	Runs	HS	Ave	100	50	Ct
Other Surrey matches	2	4	0	165	111	41.25	1	-	3
Career	209	319	50	10024	186	37.26	21	50	234

Bowling	O	M	R	W	BB	Ave	5i
Other Surrey matches	46	8	131	5	3-48	26.20	-
Career (6 ball)	569.1	96	1821	56	6-70	33.10	1

1959/60 - MCC in the West Indies

Barrington made his first overseas tour for England to the West Indies with a "new" team captained by Peter May. Promoted to no 3, he scored his first Test century in Bridgetown. In the infamous Second Test at Port-of-Spain, spoilt by crowd riots, Barrington scored his second Test century followed by 49 in the second innings to assist England to win by 256 runs. It was in this series that excessive short pitched bowling by fast bowlers came to the fore and Barrington predicted that one day crash helmets would be worn by batsmen. The remaining Test Matches were drawn so England won the series with Barrington averaging 46.66.

	Own	Team Total	O	M	R	W		Opp Total	Ct
210. MCC v Windward Islands, Grenada, December 21, 22, 23 (MCC won by ten wickets)									
b T.Redhead	9	121	5.2	3	6	2	O.Jackson c R.Subba Row F.O.Mason c G.Pullar	89	
did not bat	-	39-0	-	-	-	-		69	1
211. MCC v Barbados, Bridgetown, December 30, 31, January 1, 2 (Barbados won by ten wickets)									
b C.C.Griffith	79	238	17	2	58	1	S.M.Nurse b	533-5d	
lbw b E.de C.Weekes	79	352	-	-	-	-		58-0	
212. ENGLAND v WEST INDIES, Bridgetown, January 6, 7, 8, 9, 11, 12 (Match drawn)									
c F.C.M.Alexander b S.Ramadhin	128	482	18	3	60	1	C.C.Hunte c R.Swetman	563-8d	
did not bat	-	71-0							
213. MCC v Trinidad, Port-of-Spain, January 15, 16, 18, 19 (MCC won by six wickets)									
c A.Corneal b B.Peters	1	171-9d	7	1	17	0		301-9d	2
st M.Minshall b C.K.Singh	16	262-4	10.1	3	23	2	N.S.Asgarali c R.Illingworth K.Furlonge st K.V.Andrew	131-6d	
214. MCC v Trinidad, Point-a-Pierre, January 21, 22, 23 (MCC won by ten wickets)									
c M.C.Carew b M.Aleong	8	337-9d	15	1	63	1	B.A.Davis b	166	1
not out	2	2-0	14.5	4	42	3	B.A.Davis c M.J.K.Smith M.Olton c P.B.H.May O.Corbie lbw	172	
215. ENGLAND v WEST INDIES, Queens Park Oval, Port-of-Spain, January 28, 29, 30, February 1, 2, 3 (England won by 256 runs)									
c F.C.M.Alexander b W.W.Hall	121	382	16	10	15	0		112	1
c F.C.M.Alexander b W.W.Hall	49	230-9d	25.5	13	34	2	C.K.Singh c and b C.D.Watson c D.A.Allen	244	1
216. MCC v Jamaica, Melbourne Park, February 10, 11, 12, 13 (Match drawn)									
c V.R.Lumsden b A.L.Valentine	30	525-6d	9.5	0	44	2	L.C.Mullings lbw C.D.Watson st K.V.Andrew	374	1
			14	4	48	0		202-7	
217. ENGLAND v WEST INDIES, Kingston, February 17, 18, 19, 20, 22, 23 (Match drawn)									
c F.C.M.Alexander b C.D.Watson	16	277	21	7	38	1	D.A.St J.McMorris b	353	
lbw b J.S.Solomon	4	305	4	4	0	0		175-6	
218. MCC v Leeward Islands, Antigua, February 25, 26, 27 (Match drawn)									
lbw b E.Matthew	83	456-6d	24.4	4	56	1	H.Turner b	296	
			8	1	27	0		199-3	

219. ENGLAND v WEST INDIES, Georgetown, March 9, 10, 11, 12, 14, 15 (Match drawn)
c C.L.Walcott
    b G.St A.Sobers   27   295   6   2   22   0   402-8d
c C.L.Walcott
    b F.M.M.Worrell   0   334-8d
220. MCC v Berbice, Blairmont, March 18, 19, 21 (Match drawn)
    b L.Benjamin   103   641-6   5   0   18   0   387-2d
221. ENGLAND v WEST INDIES, Port-of-Spain, March 25, 26, 28, 29, 30, 31 (Match drawn)
c F.C.M.Alexander
    b S.Ramadhin   69   393   8   0   21   0   338-8d
c D.A.St.J.McMorris
    b G.St A.Sobers   6   350-7d   8   2   27   1   C.L.Walcott c J.M.Parks   209-5

SEASON'S AVERAGES

Batting and Fielding	M	I	NO	Runs	HS	Ave	100	50	Ct
Test matches	5	9	0	420	128	46.66	2	1	2
Other matches	7	10	1	410	103	45.55	1	3	5
Season	12	19	1	830	128	46.11	3	4	7
Career	221	338	51	10854	186	37.81	24	54	241

Bowling	O	M	R	W	BB	Ave	5i
Test matches	106.5	41	217	5	2-34	43.40	-
Other matches	130.5	23	402	12	3-42	33.50	-
Season	237.4	64	619	17	3-42	36.41	-
Career (6 ball)	806.5	160	2440	73	6-70	33.42	1

1960

Barrington began the season in great style with six fifties, then a duck against Somerset was followed by a pair against Sussex. This barren patch before the First Test saw him demoted to twelfth man and he vowed "They'll never leave me out again, I'm going to see to that". He then scored 126 against Kent and came back in for the Second Test to replace the injured G.Pullar. England won the series with Barrington scoring fifties at Trent Bridge and Old Trafford. Over the season, he scored 1878 runs at an average of 42.68 despite making only two centuries.

	Own	Team Total	O	M	R	W		Opp Total	Ct
222. Surrey v Cambridge University, Fenner's, April 27, 28, 29 (Surrey won by nine wickets)									
lbw b A.Hurd	67	201						97	
did not bat	-	36-1						136	
223. Surrey v MCC, Lord's, May 4, 5, 6 (Surrey won by 99 runs)									
c H.J.Rhodes b D.A.Allen	82	308-7d	4	0	33	0		262	
not out	65	149	-	-	-	-		96	
224. Surrey v Northamptonshire, Kennington Oval, May 7, 9, 10 (Match drawn)									
c D.W.Barrick b P.J.Watts	10	347-4d	3	0	9	0		350-8d	1
lbw b P.J.Watts	8	182-7d	2	1	1	0		85-3	
225. Surrey v Worcestershire, Kennington Oval, May 11, 12 (Surrey won by an innings and 130 runs)									
c and b D.N.F.Slade	38	341-7d						127	1
								84	
226. Surrey v Lancashire, Old Trafford, May 14, 16, 17 (Match drawn)									
c K.J.Grieves b K.Higgs	93	243						285	2
not out	44	83-4						167-7d	
227. Surrey v Sussex, Kennington Oval, May 18, (19), (20) (Match drawn)									
								327-4d	
228. Surrey v Gloucestershire, Stroud, May 21, 23, 24 (Match drawn)									
b J.B.Mortimore	51	106	5	2	8	0		239	
not out	61	179-7	-	-	-	-		119-7d	

229. Surrey v Somerset, Kennington Oval, May 25, 26, 27 (Surrey won by five wickets)
    b P.B.Wight   34 251   21   4   52   1   R.T.Virgin c D.G.W.Fletcher 275   2
    c K.E.Palmer b W.E.Alley   0 220-5   2   0   6   0   195

230. Surrey v Sussex, Hove, May 28, 30, 31 (Sussex won by an innings and 39 runs)
    c D.J.Foreman
        b D.J.Mordaunt   0 158   15   0   60   0   451-5d
    b N.I.Thomson   0 254

231. Surrey v Nottinghamshire, Trent Bridge, June 4, 6, 7 (Surrey won by eight wickets)
    c N.W.Hill b B.D.Wells   1 295   7   1   40   0   362   2
    not out   13 170-2   -   -   -   -   101   1

232. Surrey v Kent, Kennington Oval, June 11, 13, 14 (Surrey won by an innings and 38 runs)
    c A.Brown b A.L.Dixon 126 343-3d   96
                                                                                 209   1

233. Surrey v Warwickshire, Edgbaston, June 15, 16, 17 (Match drawn)
    c F.C.Gardner
        b T.W.Cartwright 21 228   -   -   -   -   239
    lbw b K.Ibadulla   63 234-4d 5   2   9   0   122-4

234. Surrey v Yorkshire, Kennington Oval, June 18, 20, 21 (Yorkshire won by nine wickets)
    c J.V.Wilson b D.B.Close 4 123   18   3   53   0   434-4d
    b F.S.Trueman   62 312   -   -   -   -   4-1

235. ENGLAND v SOUTH AFRICA, Lord's, June 23, 24, 25, 27 (England won by an innings and 73 runs)
    lbw b T.L.Goddard   24 362-8d   152
                                                                                 137

236. Surrey v Oxford University, Guildford, June 29, 30, July 1 (Surrey won by four wickets)
    not out   44 245-4d 23.2 7 47 1 J.D.Piachaud c R.A.E.Tindall 242
    not out   61 182-6   10   1   43   0   181   2

237. Surrey v Kent, Blackheath, July 2, 4, 5 (Match drawn)
    c A.H.Phebey
        b D.J.Halfyard   72 315-9d   7   0   32   0   350-8d   1
    lbw b F.Ridgway   3 137-6

238. ENGLAND v SOUTH AFRICA, Trent Bridge, July 7, 8, 9, 11 (England won by eight wickets)
    c S.O'Linn b T.L.Goddard 80 287   -   -   -   -   88
    not out   1 49-2   3   1   5   0   247

239. Players v Gentlemen, Lord's, July (13), 14, 15 (Match drawn)
    did not bat   - 168-2d   -   -   -   -   108   2
    b D.M.Sayer   32 167-9   11   0   81   1   R.Subba Row c H.Horton   227-4d

240. Surrey v Yorkshire, Bramall Lane, July 16, 18, 19 (Match drawn)
    c R.Illingworth b D.Wilson 65 283-8d   196-9d
    not out   1 157-2d   82-3

241. ENGLAND v SOUTH AFRICA, Old Trafford, July (21), (22), 23, 25, 26 (Match drawn)
    b T.L.Goddard   76 260   229
    c J.H.B.Waite
        b T.L.Goddard   35 153-7d   46-0

242. Surrey v Nottinghamshire, Kennington Oval, July 30, August 1, 2 (Surrey won by ten wickets)
    b J.Cotton   11 342-4d   -   -   -   -   184   2
    not out   12 25-0   4   1   6   0   182

243. Surrey v Glamorgan, Cardiff, August 3, 4, 5 (Glamorgan won by six wickets)
    c A.J.Watkins b D.J.Shepherd 2 235   128   1
    b J.B.Evans   5 92   202-4

244. Surrey v Middlesex, Kennington Oval, August 6, 8, 9 (Middlesex won by an innings and 21 runs)
    c J.T.Murray b J.J.Warr 0 71   284-7d
    c J.T.Murray
        b C.D.Drybrough   26 192

245. Surrey v Hampshire, Southampton, August (10), (11), 12 (Match drawn)
    c and b J.D.Piachaud 46 162-9d   156-9

246. Surrey v Middlesex, Lord's, August 13, 15, 16 (Middlesex won by eight wickets)
    c R.A.Gale b F.J.Titmus 67 281   10   2   32   0   282-7d
    lbw b A.E.Moss   13 162   0.2   0   5   0   162-2

247. ENGLAND v SOUTH AFRICA, Kennington Oval, August 18, 19, 20, 22, 23 (Match drawn)
    lbw b J.E.Pothecary   1 155   419
    c P.R.Carlstein
        b A.H.McKinnon   10 479-9d   97-4

248. Surrey v Glamorgan, Kennington Oval, August 27, 29, 30 (Surrey won by an innings and 67 runs)

b J.B.Evans	52	315-7d	-	-	-	-			101	1
			1	0	4	0			137	

249. MCC v Yorkshire, Scarborough, August 31, September 1, 2 (Match drawn)

b M.J.Cowan	16	156-9d	2	2	0	0		196-9d	2
b R.Illingworth	22	127	-	-	-	-		18-2	

250. Players v Gentlemen, Scarborough, September 3, 5, 6 (Players won by 24 runs)

b A.Hurd	71	350-9d	2	1	4	0		294
st J.Brown b A.Hurd	111	221	1	0	4	0		253

251. T.N.Pearce's XI v South Africans, Scarborough, September 7, 8, 9 (South Africans won by four wickets)

b N.A.T.Adcock	19	264	14	1	67	2	R.A.McLean c E.R.Dexter C.Wesley b	304	
lbw b C.Wesley	27	231	15	0	94	2	C.Wesley c and b R.A.McLean c E.R.Dexter	192-6	1

252. The Rest v Yorkshire, Kennington Oval, September 10, 12, 13 (Yorkshire won by 137 runs)

c J.V.Wilson b F.S.Trueman	19	151	-	-	-	-		295-9d
c sub b M.J.Cowan	11	225	5	1	15	0		218-6d

SEASON'S AVERAGES

Batting and Fielding	M	I	NO	Runs	HS	Ave	100	50	Ct
Test matches	4	7	1	227	80	37.83	-	2	-
Players v Gentlemen	2	3	0	214	111	71.33	1	1	2
Championship	19	32	5	1004	126	37.18	1	9	15
Other Surrey matches	3	5	3	319	82	159.50	-	4	2
Other matches	3	6	0	114	27	19.00	-	-	3
Season	31	53	9	1878	126	42.68	2	16	22
Career	252	391	60	12732	186	38.46	26	70	263

Bowling	O	M	R	W	BB	Ave	5i
Test matches	3	1	5	0	-	-	-
Players v Gentlemen	14	1	89	1	1-81	89.00	-
Championship	100.2	16	317	1	1-52	317.00	-
Other Surrey matches	37.2	8	123	1	1-47	123.00	-
Other matches	36	4	176	4	2-67	44.00	-
Season	190.4	30	710	7	2-67	101.42	-
Career (6 ball)	997.3	190	3150	80	6-70	39.87	1

1960/61 - Commonwealth XI in South Africa

A successful short tour to South Africa with a Commonwealth XI organised by R.A.Roberts and known as "The Cavaliers" played five matches and R.Benaud, the captain, taught Barrington how to bowl the "flipper".

	Own	Team Total	O	M	R	W		Opp	Total	Ct

253. Commonwealth XI v Rhodesia, Police 'A' (Upper) Ground, Salisbury, September 17, 18, 19 (Commonwealth XI won by six wickets)

c C.T.Defteros b D.C.Napier	31	155	12	1	37	1	D.J.L.Cornwall b	241	1
b G.B.Lawrence	66	139-4	-	-	-	-		52	1

254. Commonwealth XI v Transvaal, Wanderers, Johannesburg, September 24, 26, 27 (Commonwealth XI won by ten wickets)

c A.Bacher b K.A.Walter	7	429	-	-	-	-		167
did not bat	-	13-0	13	1	44	1	P.H.Kinsley lbw	274

255. Commonwealth XI v Natal, Kingsmead, Durban, October 1, 2, 3 (Commonwealth XI won by 86 runs)

c D.J.McGlew b G.M.Griffin	4	180	-	-	-	-		135
b J.M.Cole	7	357	10	1	32	0		316

256. Commonwealth XI v Invitation XI, Wanderers, Johannesburg, October 7, 8, 10 (Commonwealth XI won by five wickets)

c J.H.B.Waite b S.Stanley	41	345-8d	10	1	45	1	H.J.Tayfield b	249	
c J.H.B.Waite b H.J.Tayfield	8	123-5	13	2	42	4	S.O'Linn c and b	218	1
							E.J.Barlow c N.C.O'Neill		
							H.J.Tayfield c J.B.Statham		
							N.A.T.Adcock c R.B.Simpson		

SEASON'S AVERAGES

Batting and Fielding	M	I	NO	Runs	HS	Ave	100	50	Ct
Other matches	4	7	0	164	66	23.42	-	1	3
Career	256	398	60	12896	186	38.15	26	71	266

Bowling	O	M	R	W	BB	Ave	5i
Other matches	58	6	200	7	4-42	28.57	-
Career (6 ball)	1055.3	196	3350	87	6-70	38.95	1

1961

In the pre-season match at Fenner's Barrington broke a toe but came back just over a week later to score a flawless 151 not out against Hampshire. In the First Test he kept wicket for a short period whilst Murray was indisposed, but when fielding at slip dropped both Lawry and Simpson. From then on, at his own request, his days as a regular slip were numbered. In the second innings of the First Test, he took part in a long partnership with Dexter to save the match. England lost at Lord's but won at Headingley. In the match at Old Trafford, England lost after letting Australia off the hook, setting up a battle at the Oval. Unfortunately, this match petered out to a draw. Barrington added 172 with R.Subba Row despite having a fractured wrist (which he did in the previous match, Surrey v Middlesex) and this was his last match for the season, where he finished top of the national averages and second in the Test averages. In a summer of frequent collapses, his reliability in the middle order could not be overestimated.

		Own Team Total	O	M	R	W		Opp Total	Ct
257. Surrey v Cambridge University, Fenner's, April 29, May 1, 2 (Match drawn)									
c R.I.Jefferson									
b M.J.L.Willard	35	290						199	
absent hurt	-	164						210-9	
258. Surrey v Hampshire, Kennington Oval, May 10, 11, 12 (Hampshire won by five wickets)									
not out	151	356-4d	15	2	36	0		190	2
did not bat	-	141-2d	6	0	32	1	H.Horton c G.A.R.Lock	310-5d	1
259. Surrey v Australians, Kennington Oval, May 13, 15, 16 (Australians won by ten wickets)									
c R.B.Simpson									
b G.D.McKenzie	4	161	6	1	31	0		341-7d	
run out	43	214	2	0	8	0		38-0	
260. Surrey v Nottinghamshire, Trent Bridge, May 20, 22, 23 (Nottinghamshire won by 28 runs)									
c C.J.Poole b I.J.Davison	75	281-7d	-	-	-	-		278	2
c C.J.Poole b C.Forbes	47	262	6	1	31	0		293-5d	2
261. Surrey v Warwickshire, Kennington Oval, May 24, 25, 26 (Match drawn)									
c M.J.K.Smith									
b J.D.Bannister	10	352-6d	3	0	8	0		228	1
not out	37	192-6d	8	3	17	0		176-4	1
262. MCC v Australians, Lord's, May 27, 29, 30 (Australians won by 63 runs)									
c and b A.K.Davidson	55	274	7	1	28	1	B.C.Booth c M.J.Horton	381-5d	1
lbw b G.D.McKenzie	35	230	3	0	21	0		181-0d	
263. Surrey v Gloucestershire, Kennington Oval, May 31, June 1, 2 (Match drawn)									
c B.J.Meyer									
b J.B.Mortimore	93	269-7d	-	-	-	-		170	1
			26	5	67	1	J.B.Mortimore st R.Swetman	311-6	1

264. Surrey v Northamptonshire, Northampton, June 3, 5 (Surrey won by 256 runs)
    b M.Ashenden   57   326   125
    did not bat   -   116-1d   61

265. ENGLAND v AUSTRALIA, Edgbaston, June 8, 9, 10, 12, 13 (Match drawn)
    c F.M.Misson
        b K.D.Mackay   21   195   516-9d 1
    not out   48   401-4

266. Surrey v Sussex, Hove, June 14, 15, 16 (Surrey won by eight wickets)
    c K.G.Suttle b N.I.Thomson 8   251-7d   5   1   18   1   L.J.Lenham c M.D.Willett   250 2
    not out   96   243-2   7   0   24   0   240

267. Surrey v Yorkshire, Kennington Oval, June 17, 19, 20 (Match drawn)
    c J.G.Binks b K.Gillhouley 17   319   -   -   -   -   84
                              20   2   69   0   395-8d 1

268. ENGLAND v AUSTRALIA, Lord's, June 22, 23, 24, 26 (Australia won by five wickets)
    c K.D.Mackay
        b A.K.Davidson   4   206   340   2
    lbw b A.K.Davidson   66   202   71-5

269. Surrey v Kent, Blackheath, July 1, 3, 4 (Match drawn)
    c R.C.Wilson b D.W.Baker 121   402-7d   6   1   27   0   400-8d 1
    lbw b D.J.Halfyard   38   167-4   5   0   36   0   261-4d 1

270. ENGLAND v AUSTRALIA, Headingley, July 6, 7, 8 (England won by eight wickets)
    c R.B.Simpson
        b A.K.Davidson   6   299   237
    did not bat   -   62-2   120

271. Surrey v Leicestershire, Kennington Oval, July 12, 13, 14 (Leicestershire won by 1 run)
    c M.R.Hallam b B.S.Boshier 6   71   92   2
    c A.Wharton b C.T.Spencer 7   201   181   1

272. Surrey v Middlesex, Kennington Oval, July 15, 16, 17 (Middlesex won by 61 runs)
    lbw b F.J.Titmus   0   207   252-7d
    b D.Bennett   1   160   176-7d 1

273. Players v Gentlemen, Lord's, July 19, 20, 21 (Players won by 172 runs)
    b C.D.Drybrough   53   203   -   -   -   -   177
    c J.M.Brearley
        b O.S.Wheatley   53   263-6d   1   0   5   0   117   1

274. Surrey v Yorkshire, Headingley, July 22, 24, 25 (Match drawn)
    c J.G.Binks b R.Illingworth 1   394-6d   12   6   32   2   P.J.Sharpe c G.A.R.Lock   269-8d
                                                               J.V.Wilson b
    not out   65   152-4d   8   0   33   1   K.Taylor c and b   141-2 1

275. ENGLAND v AUSTRALIA, Old Trafford, July 27, 28, 29, 31, August 1 (Australia won by 54 runs)
    c N.C.O'Neill
        b R.B.Simpson   78   367   190   1
    lbw b K.D.Mackay   5   201   432

276. Surrey v Australians, Kennington Oval, August 2, 3, 4 (Australians won by 255 runs)
    c L.F.Kline b F.M.Misson 12   79   209
    not out   68   100   255-9d

277. Surrey v Nottinghamshire, Kennington Oval, August 5, 7, 8 (Surrey won by 134 runs)
    c M.Hill b A.J.Corran   163   301-7d   -   -   -   -   205   1
    c B.D.Wells b C.Forbes   95   210-8d   6   1   15   1   A.J.Corran c G.A.R.Lock   172   1

278. Surrey v Lancashire, Old Trafford, August 9, 10, 11 (Match drawn)
    not out   125   277-8d   9   4   18   1   G.Clayton c G.A.R.Lock   201   2
    c K.J.Grieves b D.M.Green 40   140-5d   -   -   -   -   212-4

279. Surrey v Middlesex, Lord's, August 12, 14, 15 (Surrey won by 29 runs)
    c J.T.Murray b R.W.Hooker 17   120   149
    b C.D.Drybrough   78   259   201

280. ENGLAND v AUSTRALIA, Kennington Oval, August 17, 18, 19, 21, 22 (Match drawn)
    c A.T.W.Grout b R.A.Gaunt 53   256   494
    c N.C.O'Neill b R.Benaud 83   370-8

SEASON'S AVERAGES

Batting and Fielding	M	I	NO	Runs	HS	Ave	100	50	Ct
Test matches	5	9	1	364	83	45.50	-	4	4
Players v Gentlemen	1	2	0	106	53	53.00	-	2	1
Championship	14	24	5	1348	163	70.94	4	7	25
Other Surrey matches	3	4	1	162	68	54.00	-	1	-
Other matches	1	2	0	90	55	45.00	-	1	1
Season	24	42	7	2070	163	59.14	4	15	31
Career	280	440	67	14966	186	40.12	30	86	297

Bowling	O	M	R	W	BB	Ave	5i
Players v Gentlemen	1	0	5	0	-	-	-
Championship	142	26	463	8	2-32	57.87	-
Other Surrey matches	8	1	39	0	-	-	-
Other matches	10	1	49	1	1-28	49.00	-
Season	161	28	556	9	2-32	61.77	-
Career (6 ball)	1216.3	224	3906	96	6-70	41.11	1

1961/62 - MCC in India, Pakistan and Ceylon

In five months an under strength MCC party, led by E.R.Dexter, was earmarked to play eight Test matches and 16 other fixtures when accomodation and travel remained for the most part primitive. Faced with these spartan conditions, a number of players opted out of the venture. Barrington played in 7 Tests and 10 other matches to average over 90 in the Tests and nearly 70 over all. He was a great favourite with the crowds introducing comedy into some performances by mimicking other players such as Mackay and Sobers. His humour off the field was greatly appreciated by his team mates and the nickname of "The Colonel" was born. The series against India was lost and no longer could England afford to take a second XI to this part of the world.

		Own	Team Total	O	M	R	W		Opp Total	Ct
281. MCC v President's XI, Rawalpindi, October 13, 14, 15 (Match drawn)										
b Javed Akhtar		11	197						208	1
c Iqbal Sheikh										
b Javed Akhtar		4	154-7						195-8d	1
282. MCC v Governor's XI, Lyallpur, October 17, 18, 19 (MCC won by 29 runs)										
c Saeed Ahmed										
b Afaq Hussain		55	252	-	-	-	-		119	1
b Antab D'Souza		0	106	9	2	24	0		210	
283. ENGLAND v PAKISTAN, Lahore, October 21, 22, 24, 25, 26 (England won by five wickets)										
run out		139	380	6	0	25	0		387-9d	
lbw b Mahmood Hussain		6	209-5	-	-	-	-		200	
284. MCC v Combined Universities, Poona, October 28, 29, 30 (Match drawn)										
not out		149	417	6	2	11	0		346-9d	1
				3	0	3	2	H.Gore st G.Millman	67-3	
								J.W.Ghorpade lbw		
285. ENGLAND v INDIA, Bombay, November 11, 12, 14, 15, 16 (Match drawn)										
not out		151	500-8d	-	-	-	-		390	1
not out		52	184-5d	3	0	18	0		180-5	
286. MCC v President's XI, Hyderabad, November 18, 19, 20 (MCC won by four wickets)										
c B.K.Kunderam										
b E.A.S.Prasanna		6	261	-	-	-	-		281-5d	2
b R.F.Surti		8	184-6	13	1	53	2	M.L.Jaisimha c and b	163-5d	1
								R.F.Surti c P.H.Parfitt		
287. MCC v Rajasthan, Jaipur, November 22, 23, 24 (Match drawn)										
c Ramesh Shah										
b R.A.J.Singh		91	222-6d						268	
did not bat		-	86-2						155-6d	1

288. ENGLAND v INDIA, Kanpur, December 1, 2, 3, 5, 6 (Match drawn)
    b S.P.Gupte   21   244   467-8d
    run out   172   497-5

289. MCC v North Zone, Jullundur, December 8, 9, 10 (MCC won by nine wickets)
    did not bat   -   256-9d   7   0   18   2   Surendranath c D.R.Smith   152
                                                        Anil Khanna b
    did not bat   -   42-1   3   1   13   1   H.Ghosh b   145

290. ENGLAND v INDIA, Feroz Shah Kotla, Delhi, December 13, 14, 16, (17), (18) (Match drawn)
    not out   113   256-3   9   1   39   0   466

291. MCC v East Zone, Cuttack, December 22, 23, 24 (Match drawn)
    not out   80   261-4d   21   6   63   2   P.Roy lbw   263-8d
                                                          P.C.Podder c G.Pullar
    not out   4   227-5

292. ENGLAND v INDIA, Calcutta, December 30, 31, January 1, 3, 4 (India won by 187 runs)
    b S.A.Durani   14   212   380
    c S.A.Durani b R.B.Desai   3   233   252   1

293. MCC v South Zone, Bangalore, January 6, 7, 8 (MCC won by 37 runs)
    b G.Kasturirangan   3   193   132
    did not bat   -   192-2d   216

294. ENGLAND v INDIA, Nehru Stadium, Madras, January 10, 11, 13, 14, 15 (India won by 128 runs)
    c V.L.Manjrekar
         b S.A.Durani   20   281   428
    lbw b R.G.Nadkarni   48   209   190

295. ENGLAND v PAKISTAN, Dacca, January 19, 20, 21, 23, 24 (Match drawn)
    b A.D'Souza   84   439   11   1   39   0   393-7d   1
    did not bat   -   38-0   21   13   17   0   216

296. MCC v Combined XI, Bahawalpur, January 26, 27, 28 (Match drawn)
    b Fazal Mahmood   0   114   162
    did not bat   -   69-0

297. MCC v All Ceylon, Colombo, February 16, 17, 18 (MCC won by eight wickets)
    b A.Fuard   93   284   210
    not out   2   72-2   144   1

SEASON'S AVERAGES

Batting and Fielding	M	I	NO	Runs	HS	Ave	100	50	Ct
Test matches	7	12	3	823	172	91.44	4	2	3
Other matches	10	14	4	506	149*	50.60	1	4	9
Season	17	26	7	1329	172	69.94	5	6	12
Career	297	466	74	16295	186	41.56	35	92	309

Bowling	O	M	R	W	BB	Ave	5i
Test matches	50	15	138	0	-	-	-
Other matches	62	12	185	9	2-3	20.55	-
Season	112	27	323	9	2-3	35.88	-
Career (6 ball)	1328.3	251	4229	105	6-70	40.66	1

1962

An attack of tonsilitis delayed Barrington's start to the season and left him short of practice for the First Test at Edgbaston. He "came good" for Surrey with centuries in three consecutive matches during June, having been discarded for the Test match at Trent Bridge. A good season for Surrey lifted his season's average to nearly 50, scoring 1865 runs at 49.07.

	Own Team	O	M	R	W		Opp	Ct
	Total						Total	

298. Surrey v Glamorgan, Kennington Oval, May 19, 21, 22 (Surrey won by an innings and 73 runs)
    c E.J.Lewis b P.M.Walker   3   339-9d   154
                                                                               112   1

299. Surrey v Lancashire, Kennington Oval, May 23, 24, 25 (Surrey won by ten wickets)

lbw b T.Greenhough	56	278-2d						200	1
did not bat	-	132-0						207	

300. Surrey v Northamptonshire, Kennington Oval, May 26, 28, 29 (Match drawn)

c K.V.Andrew b P.D.Watts	27	179						253-8d	
did not bat	-	52-0						181-9d	1

301. ENGLAND v PAKISTAN, Edgbaston, May 31, June 1, 2, 4 (England won by an innings and 24 runs)

lbw b Mahmood Hussain	9	544-5d	2	2	0	0		246	1
	-	-	-	-	-	-		274	

302. Surrey v Pakistanis, Kennington Oval, June 6, 7, 8 (Pakistanis won by 92 runs)

c and b Nasim-ul-Ghani	3	348-9d	7	0	36	0		388-6d	
c Alim-ud-Din b Munir Malik	13	185	-	-	-	-		237-4d	1

303. Surrey v Nottinghamshire, Trent Bridge, June 9, 11, 12 (Surrey won by 156 runs)

not out	26	380-5d	-	-	-	-		224	
not out	102	187-2d	1	0	7	0		187	1

304. Surrey v Lancashire, Old Trafford, June 13, 14, 15 (Lancashire won by six wickets)

c G.Clayton b T.Greenhough	29	115	-	-	-	-		124	2
c and b R.W.Barber	101	239	2.1	1	7	0		234-6	

305. Surrey v Essex, Kennington Oval, June 16, 18, 19 (Match drawn)

not out	130	352-1d	-	-	-	-			139	
not out	21	132-2d	11	2	43	1	B.R.Knight c M.J.Stewart	279-8	1

306. ENGLAND v PAKISTAN, Lord's, June 21, 22, 23 (England won by nine wickets)

c Imtiaz Ahmed b Mohammad Farooq	0	370	-	-	-	-		100	
did not bat	-	86-1	1	0	8	0		355	

307. Surrey v Oxford University, Guildford, June 27, 28 (Surrey won by an innings and 82 runs)

c M.A.Baig b N.L.Majendie	146	475-7d	3	0	14	1	J.L.Cuthbertson c P.B.H.May	214	1
			5	1	23	0		179	1

308. Surrey v Yorkshire, Bramall Lane, June 30, July 2, 3 (Match drawn)

st J.G.Binks b K.Taylor	18	218						317-4d	
c J.B.Bolus b D.Wilson	23	333-7							

309. ENGLAND v PAKISTAN, Headingley, July 5, 6, 7 (England won by an innings and 117 runs)

c Mushtaq Mohammed b Mohammad Farooq	1	428	-	-	-	-		131	1
			1	0	4	0		180	1

310. Surrey v Sussex, Kennington Oval, July 11, 12, 13 (Sussex won by 10 runs)

c K.G.Suttle b N.I.Thomson	5	184						158	1
run out	89	216						252	

311. Surrey v Gloucestershire, Gloucester, July 14, 16, 17 (Surrey won by seven wickets)

c R.C.White b J.B.Mortimore	57	284-9d						128	
not out	12	52-3						205	

312. Surrey v Somerset, Kennington Oval, July 18, 19, 20 (Match drawn)

lbw b W.E.Alley	48	198						222	
b W.E.Alley	34	129-2						255-6d	

313. Surrey v Kent, Blackheath, July 21, 23, 24 (Match drawn)

c B.W.Luckhurst b D.J.Halfyard	76	275						198	
c B.W.Luckhurst b D.W.Baker	18	176-9						336-8d	

314. Surrey v Worcestershire, Kennington Oval, July 25, (26), 27 (Match drawn)

c R.G.Broadbent b J.A.Standen	19	190-5						133	

315. Surrey v Middlesex, Kennington Oval, July 28, 30, 31 (Surrey won by 151 runs)

c C.D.Drybrough b A.E.Moss	63	287	-	-	-	-		163	1
not out	91	236-2d	6	2	25	0		209	2

316. Surrey v Worcestershire, Worcester, August 1, 2, 3 (Match drawn)

b L.J.Coldwell	8	146						169	
st R.Booth b D.N.F.Slade	27	170							

317. Surrey v Nottinghamshire, Kennington Oval, August 4, 6, (7) (Match drawn)
    lbw b J.Cotton   1   233   86-1

318. Surrey v Derbyshire, Kennington Oval, August 8, 9, 10 (Surrey won by five wickets)
    c I.R.Buxton b D.C.Morgan 31   126   160   1
    b E.Smith   9   154-5   119

319. Surrey v Middlesex, Lord's, August 11, 13, (14) (Match drawn)
    lbw b F.J.Titmus   16   319-7d   260   1
    did not bat   -   3-0

320. ENGLAND v PAKISTAN, Kennington Oval, August 16, 17, 18, 20 (England won by ten wickets)
    not out   50   480-5d   -   -   -   -   183
    did not bat   -   27-0   2   0   10   0   323

321. Surrey v Essex, Leyton, August 22, 23, 24 (Match drawn)
    lbw b T.E.Bailey   27   164   114
    not out   62   185-2d   201-7   1

322. Surrey v Yorkshire, Kennington Oval, August 25, 27, 28 (Match drawn)
    b F.S.Trueman   2   172   4.2   0   25   2 D.Wilson c P.B.H.May   416
                                                              M.Ryan c D.A.D.Sydenham
    c D.Wilson b M.Ryan   8   61-7   113-4d

323. Surrey v Hampshire, Southampton, August 29, 30, 31 (Match drawn)
    c D.A.Livingstone
        b P.J.Sainsbury   26   363-9d   6   0   27   0   358
    c H.Horton b M.D.Burden   45   258-7d   6   2   21   0   209-7

324. MCC v Yorkshire, Scarborough, September 1, 3, 4 (Match drawn)
    c J.G.Binks b R.A.Hutton   55   322-6d   -   -   -   -   338-9d
    c J.G.Binks b D.Wilson   107   232-8d   5   0   11   1 J.V.Wilson c K.V.Andrew   107-6

325. T.N.Pearce's XI v Pakistanis, Scarborough, September 5, 6, 7 (Pakistanis won by five wickets)
    lbw b Nasim-ul-Ghani   46   279-7d   162-6d
    did not bat   -   97-1d   215-5   1

326. Players v Gentlemen, Scarborough, September 8, 10, 11 (Players won by seven wickets)
    b C.D.Drybrough   100   337   17   1   87   1 D.Kirby c and b   328   1
    b C.D.Drybrough   25   212-3   -   -   -   -   217   2

SEASON'S AVERAGES

Batting and Fielding	M	I	NO	Runs	HS	Ave	100	50	Ct
Test matches	4	4	1	60	50*	20.00	-	1	3
Players v Gentlemen	1	2	0	125	100	62.50	1	-	3
Championship	20	34	7	1310	130*	48.51	3	7	14
Other Surrey matches	2	3	0	162	146	54.00	1	-	3
Other matches	2	3	0	208	107	69.33	1	1	1
Season	29	46	8	1865	146	49.07	6	9	24
Career	326	512	82	18160	186	42.23	41	101	333

Bowling	O	M	R	W	BB	Ave	5i
Test matches	6	2	22	0	-	-	-
Players v Gentlemen	17	1	87	1	1-57	87.00	-
Championship	36.3	7	155	3	2-25	51.66	-
Other Surrey matches	15	1	73	1	1-14	73.00	-
Other matches	5	0	11	1	1-11	11.00	-
Season	79.3	11	348	6	2-25	58.00	-
Career (6 ball)	1408	262	4577	111	6-70	41.60	1

1962/63 - MCC in Australia

At Adelaide, Barrington scored 104 against South Australia followed by his first ever double century, 219 against an Australian XI at Melbourne. This was followed by 183 not out against Queensland at Brisbane.The First Test was drawn, England won at Melbourne and lost at Sydney. Both sides played safe in a dull draw at Adelaide, although Barrington, promoted to no 3, facing Davidson in full flow hit him for four successive boundaries. So angry was Davidson that he gave everything to the next ball only to tear fibres from his hamstring muscle. He was unable to bowl again in the match. The series depended on the last match at Sydney but the match petered out in a draw on an unsuitable pitch. Barrington's century in the first innings contained only four boundaries. His return of 582 runs in the series was the best since W.R.Hammond.

		Own Team Total	O	M	R	W		Opp Total	Ct

327. MCC v Western Australia, Perth, October 19, 20, 22 (MCC won by ten wickets)

Batting	Score	Own Team Total	O	M	R	W	Bowling	Opp Total	Ct
c H.G.Bevan b D.E.Hoare	24	303	-	-	-	-		77	
did not bat	-	49-0	10	1	47	0		274	

328. MCC v Combined XI, Perth, October 26, 27, 29, 30 (Combined XI won by ten wickets)

Batting	Score	Own Team Total	O	M	R	W	Bowling	Opp Total	Ct
c B.L.Buggins b G.D.McKenzie	0	157	2	0	8	0		317	1
c M.T.Vernon b D.E.Hoare	44	270	4	0	35	0		115-0	

329. MCC v South Australia, Adelaide, November 2, 3, 5, 6 (Match drawn)

Batting	Score	Own Team Total	O	M	R	W	Bowling	Opp Total	Ct
c B.N.Jarman b N.J.N.Hawke	104	508-9d	4	0	27	0		335	
did not bat	-	95-1	-	-	-	-		283-7d	

330. MCC v Australian XI, Melbourne, November 9, 10, 12, 13 (Match drawn)

Batting	Score	Own Team Total	O	M	R	W	Bowling	Opp Total	Ct
not out	219	633-7d						451	
c F.M.Misson b T.R.Veivers	19	68-5d						201-4	1

331. MCC v Queensland, Brisbane, November 23, 24, 26, 27 (Match drawn)

Batting	Score	Own Team Total	O	M	R	W	Bowling	Opp Total	Ct
not out	183	581-6d	8	1	71	1	D.G.Hughson lbw	433-7d	
			12	3	28	0		94-7	

332. ENGLAND v AUSTRALIA, Brisbane, November 30, December 1, 3, 4, 5 (Match drawn)

Batting	Score	Own Team Total	O	M	R	W	Bowling	Opp Total	Ct
c P.J.P.Burge b R.Benaud	78	389	12	3	44	1	A.K.Davidson c F.S.Trueman	404	1
c G.D.McKenzie b A.K.Davidson	23	278-6	-	-	-	-		362-4d	

333. MCC v South Australia, Adelaide, December 23, 24, 26, 27 (Match drawn)

Batting	Score	Own Team Total	O	M	R	W	Bowling	Opp Total	Ct
run out	52	586-5d	18	2	55	3	G.St A.Sobers c D.A.Allen / H.N.Dansie c and b / J.F.Sangster c P.H.Parfitt	450	2
not out	52	167-6d	-	-	-	-		113-4	

334. ENGLAND v AUSTRALIA, Melbourne, December 29, 31, January 1, 2, 3 (England won by seven wickets)

Batting	Score	Own Team Total	O	M	R	W	Bowling	Opp Total	Ct
lbw b G.D.McKenzie	35	331	6	0	23	0		316	2
not out	0	237-3	5	0	22	0		248	

335. MCC v Combined XI, Launceston, January 4, 5, 7 (MCC won by 313 runs)

Batting	Score	Own Team Total	O	M	R	W	Bowling	Opp Total	Ct
c K.J.Aldridge b B.C.Patterson	73	331-7d	2.4	1	16	1	K.J.Aldridge st J.T.Murray	77	
did not bat	-	116-1d	2	0	8	1	K.J.Aldridge c D.S.Sheppard	57	

336. ENGLAND v AUSTRALIA, Sydney, January 11, 12, 14, 15 (Australia won by eight wickets)

Batting	Score	Own Team Total	O	M	R	W	Bowling	Opp Total	Ct
lbw b A.K.Davidson	35	279	8	0	43	0		319	1
b G.D.McKenzie	21	104	-	-	-	-		67-2	

337. ENGLAND v AUSTRALIA, Adelaide, January 25, 26, 28, 29, 30 (Match drawn)

Batting	Score	Own Team Total	O	M	R	W	Bowling	Opp Total	Ct
b R.B.Simpson	63	331						393	
not out	132	223-4						293	2

338. MCC v Victoria, Melbourne, February 1, 2, 4, 5 (Match drawn)

Batting	Score	Own Team Total	O	M	R	W	Bowling	Opp Total	Ct
c R.M.Cowper b C.Guest	33	375	2.6	0	14	1	A.N.Connolly c P.H.Parfitt	307	
c R.C.Jordon b I.Meckiff	66	218-5d	17	3	60	2	R.C.Jordon c and b / I.Meckiff c L.J.Coldwell	188-9	1

339. ENGLAND v AUSTRALIA, Sydney, February 15, 16, 18, 19, 20 (Match drawn)

Batting	Score	Own Team Total	O	M	R	W	Bowling	Opp Total	Ct
c R.N.Harvey b R.Benaud	101	321	-	-	-	-		349	
c A.T.W.Grout b G.D.McKenzie	94	268-8d	8	3	22	0		152-4	

SEASON'S AVERAGES

Batting and Fielding	M	I	NO	Runs	HS	Ave	100	50	Ct
Test matches	5	10	2	582	132*	72.75	2	3	6
Other matches	8	12	3	869	219*	96.55	3	4	6
Season	13	22	5	1451	219*	85.35	5	7	12
Career	339	534	87	19611	219*	43.87	46	108	345

Bowling	O	M	R	W	BB	Ave	5i
Test matches	39	6	154	1	1-44	154.00	-
Other matches	82.2	11	369	9	3-53	41.00	-
Season	121.2	17	523	10	3-53	52.30	-
Career (6 ball)	1408	262 ⎫	5100	121	6-70	42.14	1
Career (8 ball)	121.2	17 ⎭					

1962/63 - MCC in New Zealand

A successful tour in New Zealand gave him an overall tour aggregate of 1763 (Avge 80.13), which was only 18 runs short of the 1781 scored by D.C.S.Compton in South Africa in 1948/49.

	Own Team Total	O	M	R	W		Opp Total	Ct

340. ENGLAND v NEW ZEALAND, Auckland, February 23, 25, 26, 27 (England won by an innings and 215 runs)

| c W.R.Playle b F.J.Cameron | 126 | 562-7d | 12 | 4 | 38 | 0 | | 258 | |
| | | | - | - | - | - | | 89 | 1 |

341. ENGLAND v NEW ZEALAND, Wellington, March 1, 2, 4 (England won by an innings and 47 runs)

c A.E.Dick b J.R.Reid	76	428	2.3	1	1	1	F.J.Cameron lbw	194	
			11	3	32	3	B.W.Sinclair c and b	187	3
							M.J.F.Shrimpton c P.H.Parfitt		
							F.J.Cameron lbw		

342. MCC v Otago Invitation XI, Dunedin, March 8, 9, 11 (MCC won by an innings and 10 runs)

lbw b F.J.Cameron	18	296-9d	-	-	-	-		116	
			10	2	41	3	R.Hendry c F.J.Titmus	170	
							J.C.Alabaster lbw		
							J.Hill lbw		

343. ENGLAND v NEW ZEALAND, Christchurch, March 15, 16, 18, 19 (England won by seven wickets)

| lbw b R.C.Motz | 47 | 253 | 5 | 0 | 18 | 0 | | 266 | 1 |
| c J.R.Reid b R.W.Blair | 45 | 173-3 | - | - | - | - | | 159 | |

SEASON'S AVERAGES

Batting and Fielding	M	I	NO	Runs	HS	Ave	100	50	Ct
Test matches	3	4	0	294	126	73.50	1	1	5
Other matches	1	1	0	18	18	18.00	-	-	-
Season	4	5	0	312	126	62.40	1	1	5
Career	343	539	87	19923	219*	44.07	47	109	350

Bowling	O	M	R	W	BB	Ave	5i
Test matches	30.3	8	89	4	3-32	22.25	-
Other matches	10	2	41	3	3-41	13.66	-
Season	40.3	10	130	7	3-32	18.57	-
Career (6 ball)	1448.3	272 ⎫	5230	128	6-70	40.85	1
Career (8 ball)	121.2	17 ⎭					

1963

Barrington scored a century for Surrey against the visiting West Indians but England were soundly beaten at Old Trafford in the First Test. A dramatic match at Lord's was drawn with plucky defence by Barrington in the second innings culminating with Cowdrey batting in the last over despite a broken arm. England won at Edgbaston handsomely although Barrington had a poor game being dismissed twice by Sobers playing on to balls outside the off stump. England lost at Headingley, at one stage in the first innings being 34-5 following a devastating spell by Griffith. In the Oval Test match, Barrington attacked Griffith but fell in a trap when, expecting another bouncer, he was bowled by a fast swinging yorker. For Barrington, the series had been a bitter disappointment. For the whole season, he averaged over 40 with the bat. In the last match of the season against Warwickshire his 51 not out was made with only 13 scoring strokes, a Surrey record, being 3 sixes, 7 fours, 1 three and 2 singles.

	Own Team Total	O	M	R	W		Opp Total	Ct
344. Surrey v MCC, Lord's, May (1), (2), 3 (Match drawn)								
b T.E.Bailey	4	144-6					143	
345. Surrey v Kent, Kennington Oval, May 4, 6, 7 (Surrey won by nine wickets)								
c S.E.Leary b D.M.Sayer	30	201	7	2	13	1	M.H.Denness b	196	1
not out	39	66-1	-	-	-	-		67	2
346. Surrey v Derbyshire, Kennington Oval, May 8, 9, 10 (Surrey won by an innings and 6 runs)								
b I.R.Buxton	48	343-7d	-	-	-	-		175	
			6	1	16	1	W.F.Oates c R.A.E.Tindall	162	
347. Surrey v Leicestershire, Kennington Oval, May 11, 13, 14 (Match drawn)								
not out	94	255-3d					166	1
							140-5	
348. Surrey v Worcestershire, Worcester, May 15, 16, 17 (Match drawn)								
run out	8	262	-	-	-	-		159	
c J.A.Standen b M.J.Horton	38	195	9	6	11	0		205-6	1
349. Surrey v Essex, Kennington Oval, May 18, 19, 20 (Match drawn)								
lbw b K.C.Preston	95	320-4d	-	-	-	-		310	1
c R.N.S.Hobbs b P.J.Phelan	7	197-4d	6	2	12	2	B.E.A.Edmeades b	40-4	1
							P.J.Phelan c and b		
350. Surrey v West Indians, Kennington Oval, May 25, 27, (28) (Match drawn)								
not out	110	195	7	2	20	0		191	
			-	-	-	-		145-1	
351. Surrey v Nottinghamshire, Trent Bridge, June 1, 3, 4 (Nottinghamshire won by 115 runs)								
c and b C.Forbes	2	151	8	1	24	0		375-8d	
st G.Millman b B.D.Wells	25	236	-	-	-	-		127-8d	
352. ENGLAND v WEST INDIES, Old Trafford, June 6, 7, 8, 10 (West Indies won by ten wickets)								
c D.L.Murray b W.W.Hall	16	205					501-6d	
b L.R.Gibbs	8	296					1-0	
353. Surrey v Hampshire, Kennington Oval, June 15, 17, 18 (Hampshire won by six wickets)								
c A.C.D.Ingleby-MacKenzie								
b D.Shackleton	20	179					164	
c and b A.R.Wassell	17	114					131-4	
354. ENGLAND v WEST INDIES, Lord's, June 20, 21, 22, 24, 25 (Match drawn)								
c G.St A.Sobers								
b F.M.M.Worrell	80	297					301	1
c D.L.Murray b C.C.Griffith	60	228					229	
355. Surrey v Sussex, Guildford, June 26, 27 (Surrey won by nine wickets)								
st J.M.Parks b R.V.Bell	77	238-7d					111	1
did not bat	-	14-1					137	1
356. Surrey v Leicestershire, Ashby de la Zouch, June (29), July 1, 2 (Match drawn)								
c R.Julian b J.S.Savage	5	47-3d					49-2d	
c R.L.Pratt b J.S.Savage	1	154					34-2	
357. ENGLAND v WEST INDIES, Edgbaston, July 4, 5, 6, 8, 9 (England won by 217 runs)								
b G.St A.Sobers	9	216					186	
b G.St A.Sobers	1	278-9d					91	1
358. Surrey v Yorkshire, Kennington Oval, July 13, 15, 16 (Match drawn)								
not out	84	168-4d					149	
did not bat	-	19-0					180-6d	1
359. MCC Australian Touring Team v The Rest, Lord's, July 17, 18, 19 (The Rest won by two wickets)								
b D.Shackleton	23	221	-	-	-	-		117	
c M.J.Stewart b K.E.Palmer	1	72-7d	1	0	4	1	J.M.Parks b	179-8	
360. Surrey v Yorkshire, Bramall Lane, July 20, 22, 23 (Match drawn)								
c J.G.Binks b A.G.Nicholson	2	225	1	0	16	0		246	
not out	79	230-3d	-	-	-	-		21-4	
361. ENGLAND v WEST INDIES, Headingley, July 25, 26, 27, 29 (West Indies won by 221 runs)								
c F.M.M.Worrell								
b L.R.Gibbs	25	174					397	1
lbw b G.St A.Sobers	32	231					229	

362. Surrey v West Indians, Kennington Oval, July 31, August 1, 2 (Match drawn)
    c D.W.Allan b L.A.King   43   311   183
    run out   22   196-4d   253-8d

363. Surrey v Nottinghamshire, Kennington Oval, August 3, 5, 6 (Match drawn)
    c I.J.Davison b B.D.Wells   53   314-5d   25   8   40   4   N.B.Whittingham b   217
                                                                G.Millman c N.L.Majendie
                                                                K.Gillhouley c A.B.D. Parsons
                                                                R.T.Simpson c R.Harman
    did not bat   -   18-1

364. Surrey v Hampshire, Southampton, August 7, 8, 9 (Match drawn)
    lbw b D.Shackleton   76   190   178
    not out   100   232-7   253-6d

365. Surrey v Middlesex, Kennington Oval, August 10, 12, 13 (Surrey won by eight wickets)
    c J.S.E.Price b R.W.Hooker 75   210   -   -   -   -   183-8d
    did not bat   -   130-2   5   3   4   0   155

366. Surrey v Lancashire, Kennington Oval, August 14, 15, (16) (Match drawn)
    b J.B.Statham   8   226-9d   2   1   7   0   229-8d   2
    did not bat   -   41-1

367. Surrey v Essex, Clacton-on-Sea, August 17, 19, 20 (Match drawn)
    b B.E.A.Edmeades   9   277-7d   218
                                                    182-8   1

368. ENGLAND v WEST INDIES, Kennington Oval, August 22, 23, 24, 26 (West Indies won by eight wickets)
    c G.St A.Sobers b L.R.Gibbs16   275   246
    b C.C.Griffith   28   223   255-8

369. Surrey v Somerset, Kennington Oval, August 28, 29, 30 (Surrey won by 204 runs)
    c H.W.Stephenson
              b G.H.Hall   15   200   142   1
    c H.W.Stephenson
              b F.E.Rumsey 26   257-4d   111   1

370. Surrey v Middlesex, Lord's, August 31, September 2, 3 (Match drawn)
    b F.J.Titmus   6   149   224-7d
    b F.J.Titmus   0   239-7d   161-5

371. Surrey v Warwickshire, Kennington Oval, September (4), 5, (6) (Match drawn)
    not out   51   148-2d   140-6d
                                                    14-0

SEASON'S AVERAGES

Batting and Fielding	M	I	NO	Runs	HS	Ave	100	50	Ct
Test matches	5	10	0	275	80	27.50	-	2	3
Championship	19	29	6	1090	100*	47.39	1	9	15
Other Surrey matches	3	4	1	179	110*	59.66	1	-	-
Other matches	1	2	0	24	23	12.00	-	-	-
Season	28	45	7	1568	110*	41.26	2	11	18
Career	371	584	94	21491	219*	43.85	49	120	368

Bowling	O	M	R	W	BB	Ave	5i
Championship	69	24	143	8	4-40	17.87	-
Other Surrey matches	7	2	20	0	-	-	-
Other matches	1	0	4	1	1-4	4.00	-
Season	77	26	167	9	4-40	18.55	-
Career (6 ball)	1525.3	298 }	5397	137	6-70	39.39	1
Career (8 ball)	121.2	17					

1963/64 - MCC in India

After defying India with a long slow innings in the First Test when England had trouble fielding eleven fit men, Barrington broke a finger in the match against West Zone and this was serious enough to rule him out for the rest of the tour.

	Own Team Total	O	M	R	W		Opp Total	Ct
372. MCC v President's XI, Bangalore, January 3, 4, 5 (Match drawn)								
not out	76 272-3d	8	2	16	0		298-4d	
did not bat	- 259-6							
373. MCC v South Zone, Hyderabad, January 6, 7, 8 (MCC won by an innings and 27 runs)								
c sub b Mahendar Kamur 108 480		5.2	2	11	3	A.A.Baig c P.J.Sharpe	140	1
						D.Kameth hit wkt		
						Habeeb Khan b		
		14	4	45	2	A.G.Milka Singh		
						c M.J.Stewart	313	
						Habeeb Khan lbw		
374. ENGLAND v INDIA, Nehru Stadium, Madras, January 10, 11, 12, 14, 15 (Match drawn)								
c and b C.G.Borde	80 317	4	0	23	0		457-7d	
did not bat	- 241-5	2	0	6	0		152-9d	
375. MCC v West Zone, Ahmedabad, January 17, 18, 19 (Match drawn)								
lbw b R.F.Surti	72 400-5d	1.3	1	1	1	B.P.Gupte c J.M.Parks	208	
		5	0	29	1	N.J.Contractor c and b	282-3	1

SEASON'S AVERAGES

Batting and Fielding	M	I	NO	Runs	HS	Ave	100	50	Ct
Test matches	1	1	0	80	80	80.00	-	1	-
Other matches	3	3	1	256	108	128.00	1	2	2
Season	4	4	1	336	108	112.00	1	3	2
Career	375	588	95	21827	219*	44.27	50	123	370

Bowling	O	M	R	W	BB	Ave	5i
Test matches	6	0	29	0	-	-	-
Other matches	33.5	9	102	7	3-11	14.57	-
Season	39.5	9	131	7	3-11	18.71	-
Career (6 ball)	1565.2	307 ⎫	5528	144	6-70	38.38	1
Career (8 ball)	121.2	17 ⎭					

1964

In his benefit year, Barrington had great help from his wife, Ann, whose secretarial skills and financial training was invaluable. In the Test matches against Australia, bad weather at Trent Bridge and Lord's made draws inevitable. At Headingley, Barrington was dismissed for 29 in the first innings continuing a bad trot for England at home with precisely 200 runs in his last ten innings with a highest score of 33. In the second innings, facing a deficit of 121, he came out to partner J.H.Edrich and went for his shots making 85 before being given out lbw to Vievers, a decision even the Australians thought harsh. Australia won the match and on a docile pitch at Old Trafford, Australia scored 659-8 in their first innings. Barrington joined Dexter coming in at no 4 and by the Monday morning England still needed 295 to avoid the follow-on. Despite alarms, Dexter and Barrington put on 246 and eventually Barrington scored 256 batting for 11 hours 25 minutes. In his next first class match, he scored 207 against Nottinghamshire at the Oval. His benefit match was against Yorkshire – it raised £10,702 - and despite some controversy, was financially successful and at the end of the season, he finished top of the averages.

	Own Team Total	O	M	R	W		Opp Total	Ct
376. Surrey v MCC, Lord's, May 2, 4, 5 (Match drawn)								
lbw b B.R.Knight	55 200-9d	14	3	46	5	K.W.R Fletcher c S.J.Storey	210	
						K.E.Palmer b		
						D.N.F.Slade b		
						J.G.Binks b		
						R.N.S.Hobbs c M.J.Stewart		
c J.S.E.Price b R.N.S.Hobbs 23 193-7		7	1	35	0		183-1d	

377. Surrey v Northamptonshire, Kennington Oval, May 20, 21, 22 (Match drawn)
    c M.E.J.C.Norman
        b J.D.F.Larter   43   319   6   0   27   0   275-6d
    c B.L.Reynolds
        b J.D.F.Larter   14   116-5d   -   -   -   -   60-4

378. Surrey v Leicestershire, Kennington Oval, May 23, 25, 26 (Match drawn)
    c R.L.Pratt b B.S.Boshier   24   212   3   0   10   0   190
    c T.Thompson b R.C.Smith   19   125-8 4   1   12   0   221-9d   1

379. Surrey v Kent, Gravesend, May 30, June (1), 2 (Match drawn)
    not out   150   339-5d   155

380. ENGLAND v AUSTRALIA, Trent Bridge, June 4, 5, (6), 8, 9 (Match drawn)
    c W.M.Lawry b T.R.Veivers   22   216-8d   168   2
    lbw b G.E.Corling   33   193-9d   40-2

381. Surrey v Worcestershire, Kennington Oval, June 10, 11, 12 (Match drawn)
    lbw b L.J.Coldwell   0   253   253
    not out   136   236-3d   216-8   1

382. Surrey v Essex, Kennington Oval, June 13, 15, 16 (Match drawn)
    c R.N.S.Hobbs b P.H.Phelan   70   285-9d   -   -   -   -   206
    not out   50   171-3d   24   8   50   2   B.R.Knight c M.D.Willett   184-5
                                                                  K.W.R.Fletcher c S.J.Storey

383. ENGLAND v AUSTRALIA, Lord's, June (18), (19), 20, 22, 23 (Match drawn)
    lbw b G.D.McKenzie   5   246   176
                                                                                             168-4

384. Surrey v Yorkshire, Bradford, June 27, 29, 30 (Match drawn)
    c K.Taylor b R.Illingworth   76   358   -   -   -   -   273   1
                                              8.4   0   26   1   M.Ryan b   292   1

385. ENGLAND v AUSTRALIA, Headingley, July 2, 3, 4, 6 (Australia won by seven wickets)
    b G.D.McKenzie   29   268   389
    lbw b T.R.Veivers   85   229   111-3   1

386. Surrey v Derbyshire, Kennington Oval, July 8, 9, 10 (Surrey won by 170 runs)
    c R.W.Taylor b E.Smith   31   266-4d   25   7   59   4   J.F.Harvey c R.A.E.Tindall 213
                                                                  M.H.Page lbw
                                                                  T.J.P.Eyre c D.A.D.Sydenham
                                                                  R.W.Taylor st A.Long
    c E.Smith b H.L.Jackson   45   184-5d   8   3   20   0   67   1

387. Surrey v Gloucestershire, Gloucester, July 11, 13 (Surrey won by ten wickets)
    c M.Bissex b J.B.Mortimore   89   280   143   1
    did not bat   -   27-0   163   1

388. Surrey v Lancashire, Southport, July 15, 16, 17 (Match drawn)
    b K.Higgs   12   194   292-9d   1
    c K.J.Grieves b G.Pullar   68   200-4   208-7d

389. Surrey v Sussex, Hove, July 18, 20, 21 (Surrey won by ten wickets)
    not out   76   237-8d   165   1
    did not bat   -   48-0   119   2

390. ENGLAND v AUSTRALIA, Old Trafford, July 23, 24, 25, 27, 28 (Match drawn)
    lbw b G.D.McKenzie   256   611   -   -   -   -   656-8d
                                                 1   0   4   0   4-0

391. Surrey v Nottinghamshire, Kennington Oval, August 1, 3, 4 (Match drawn)
    c M.Hill b C.Forbes   207   370   7   1   16   0   249
                                                20   6   43   0   245-4

392. Surrey v Sussex, Kennington Oval, August 5, 6, 7 (Surrey won by 182 runs)
    c J.M.Parks b J.A.Snow   22   158   106
    c G.C.Cooper b M.A.Buss   13   311-5d   181

393. Surrey v Middlesex, Lord's, August 8, 10, 11 (Match drawn)
    lbw b J.S.E.Price   2   294   254-9d   1
    b F.J.Titmus   37   100-0d   7   2   11   0   85-5   1

394. ENGLAND v AUSTRALIA, Kennington Oval, August 13, 14, 15, 17, (18) (Match drawn)
    c R.B.Simpson
        b N.J.N.Hawke   47   182   379
    not out   54   381-4

395. Surrey v Warwickshire, Edgbaston, August 19, 20, 21 (Warwickshire won by an innings and 72 runs)
    b R.B.Edmonds   34   115   273-9d   1
    b R.V.Webster   1   86

396. Surrey v Yorkshire, Kennington Oval, August 22, 24, 25 (Surrey won by 57 runs)
c F.S.Trueman

b R.Illingworth	8	307		207
absent ill	-	141-8d		184

397. Surrey v Warwickshire, Kennington Oval, September 2, 3, 4 (Surrey won by an innings and 78 runs)

b R.E.Hitchcock	36	391-8d	-	-	-	-	146	2
			5	2	7	0	167	1

SEASON'S AVERAGES

Batting and Fielding	M	I	NO	Runs	HS	Ave	100	50	Ct
Test matches	5	8	1	531	256	75.85	1	2	3
Championship	16	25	4	1263	207	60.14	3	6	17
Other Surrey matches	1	2	0	78	55	39.00	-	1	-
Season	22	35	5	1872	256	62.40	4	9	20
Career	397	623	100	23699	256	45.31	54	132	390

Bowling	O	M	R	W	BB	Ave	5i
Test matches	1	0	4	0	-	-	-
Championship	117.4	30	284	7	4-59	40.57	-
Other Surrey matches	21	4	81	5	5-46	16.20	1
Season	139.4	34	369	12	5-46	30.75	1
Career (6 ball)	1705	341 }	5897	156	6-70	37.80	2
Career (8 ball)	121.2	17 }					

1964/65 - MCC in South Africa

Barrington enjoyed an excellent tour to South Africa, where England won the series 1-0. At Cape Town in the drawn Test match, he took three wickets for four runs whilst imitating Laker, his best Test match bowling figures. He captained MCC against Orange Free State when they won by seven wickets. By the end of the tour, not only did he have an excellent batting average, but finished top of the bowling averages taking 24 wickets at 7.25.

		Own Team Total	O	M	R	W		Opp Total	Ct

398. MCC v Rhodesia, Police "A" (Upper) Ground, Salisbury, October 24, 25, 26, 27 (MCC won by five wickets)

c A.de Caila b B.Bennett	74	298		281
not out	26	209-5		225

399. MCC v Transvaal, Johannesburg, November 6, 7, 9 (MCC won by an innings and 82 runs)

c A.Bacher b B.D.Thorp	169	464-9d		125
				257

400. MCC v Eastern Province, Port Elizabeth, November 20, 21, 23 (MCC won by an innings and 150 runs)

c and b E.J.Barlow	2	447-7d	-	-	-	-		133
			4.1	1	17	3	J.P.Harty b	164
							M.Burton c M.J.K.Smith	
							G.Den c D.J.Brown	

401. MCC v Western Province, Cape Town, November 27, 28, 30, December 1 (Match drawn)

not out	169	441		357
run out	82	228-6d		158-8

402. ENGLAND v SOUTH AFRICA, Durban, December 4, 5, 7, 8 (England won by an innings and 104 runs)

not out	148	485-5d		155
				226	1

403. MCC v South African Universities, Pietermaritzburg, December 12, 14, 15 (MCC won by an innings and 112 runs)

c P.H.J.Trimborn b G.Hall	6	356	10	2	29	5	B.J.Versfeld c P.H.Parfitt	114
							D.Mackay-Coghill c P.H.Parfitt	
							R.K.Muzzell c P.H.Parfitt	
							R.S.Steyn b	
							G.Hall c R.N.S.Hobbs	

| | 20 | 9 | 25 | 4 | E.V.Chatterton b | 130 |

C.Weinstein lbw
R.Dumbrill c P.H.Parfitt
D.Mackay-Coghill c J.T.Murray

404. MCC v N.E.Transvaal, Pretoria, December 18, 19, 21 (MCC won by an innings and 11 runs)

| c I.W.Baynard b G.G.Hall | 45 | 350 | - | - | - | - | | 204 | |
| | | | 1 | 0 | 1 | 0 | | 135 | 2 |

405. ENGLAND v SOUTH AFRICA, Johannesburg, December 23, 24, 26, 28, 29 (Match drawn)

c R.G.Pollock
| b P.M.Pollock | 121 | 531 | 4 | 0 | 29 | 0 | | 317 | |
| | | | - | - | - | - | | 336-6 | |

406. ENGLAND v SOUTH AFRICA, Cape Town, January 1, 2, 4, 5, 6 (Match drawn)

c D.T.Lindsay
| b P.M.Pollock | 49 | 442 | - | - | - | - | | 501-7d | |
| not out | 14 | 15-0 | 3.1 | 1 | 4 | 3 | D.T.Lindsay b | 346 | |

P.M.Pollock lbw
G.G.Hall b

407. MCC v Orange Free State, Bloemfontein, January 15, 16, 18 (MCC won by seven wickets)

c C.Richardson
| b M.J.Macauley | 3 | 199-7d | | | | | | 170 | 1 |
| not out | 34 | 143-3 | | | | | | 171-9d | 1 |

408. ENGLAND v SOUTH AFRICA, Johannesburg, January 22, 23, 25, 26, 27 (Match drawn)

| c J.H.B.Waite b E.J.Barlow | 93 | 384 | | | | | | 390-6d | |
c H.D.Bromfield
| b A.H.McKinnon | 11 | 153-6 | | | | | | 307-3d | |

409. MCC v Griqualand West, De Beers Stadium, Kimberley, January 29, 30, February 1 (MCC won by ten wickets)

c R.Scurr b B.Burrow	10	226	18	5	29	2	W.Symcox b	140	
							T.Heale c E.R.Dexter		
did not bat	-	24-0	12.5	5	40	7	A.McLachlan c M.J.K.Smith	107	

T.Heale c M.J.Brearley
A.McNamara b
B.Burrow st J.T.Murray
D.Lee c P.H.Parfitt
R.Scurr lbw
E.Engelsman c R.N.S.Hobbs

410. ENGLAND v SOUTH AFRICA, Port Elizabeth, February 12, 13, 15, 16, 17 (Match drawn)

c P.L.Van der Merwe
| b T.L.Goddard | 72 | 435 | | | | | | 502 | 2 |
| did not bat | - | 29-1 | | | | | | 178-4d | |

SEASON'S AVERAGES

Batting and Fielding	M	I	NO	Runs	HS	Ave	100	50	Ct
Test matches	5	7	2	508	148	101.60	2	2	3
Other matches	8	11	3	620	169*	77.50	2	2	4
Season	13	18	5	1128	169*	86.76	4	4	7
Career	410	641	105	24827	256	46.31	58	136	397

Bowling	O	M	R	W	BB	Ave	5i
Test matches	7.1	1	33	3	3-4	11.00	-
Other matches	66	22	141	21	7-40	6.71	2
Season	73.1	23	174	24	7-40	7.25	2
Career (6 ball)	1778.1	364 }	6171	180	7-40	34.28	4
Career (8 ball)	121.2	17 }					

1965

A slow start to the season found Barrington scoring only 177 runs in his first 12 first-class innings. Being out of form there was a powerful argument to omit him from the England team. However, he was picked for the first match against New Zealand at Edgbaston and scored a slow century.

Returning to the Oval, Herbert Strudwick, the former Surrey coach, travelled up from Brighton at his own expense, to point out technical faults in his batting that he had spotted on television. For Surrey against the New Zealanders he scored 70 and 129 not out, but he was dropped from the England team for the Lord's Test match. He was suprisingly restored to the team for the final New Zealand Test because of injuries to Boycott and Dexter and scored a sound 163 in a stand of 369 with J.H.Edrich. Against South Africa he scored 91 in a drawn match, but when South Africa won at Trent Bridge he scored only 1 in each innings. In the final Test, he scored 73 in the second innings when rain prevented England winning to square the series. Barrington appeared in his only one-day final at Lord's when Surrey were comprehensively beaten by Yorkshire.

	Own Team Total	O	M	R	W		Opp Total	Ct
411. Surrey v Cambridge University, Fenner's, April (28), 29, 30 (Surrey won by eight wickets)								
did not bat	-	79-0d					127-6d	1
not out	41	176-2					124	
412. Surrey v MCC, Lord's, May 1, 3, (4) (Match drawn)								
c R.N.S.Hobbs								
b D.L.Underwood	23	83-5					163	2
413. Surrey v Hampshire, Kennington Oval, May 5, 6, 7 (Match drawn)								
c D.Shackleton								
b A.R.Wassell	21	248					260	
b P.J.Sainsbury	3	180-7d					41-1	
414. Surrey v Warwickshire, Kennington Oval, May 8, 10, 11 (Match drawn)								
b R.B.Edmonds	7	176	1.2	0	9	2	R.B.Edmonds c R.I.Jefferson	257	1
							D.J.Brown c S.J.Storey	
b T.W.Cartwright	5	239-5d	6	2	18	0		68-2	
415. Surrey v Sussex, Hove, May 12, 13, 14 (Sussex won by seven wickets)								
lbw b A.Buss	6	325-6d					354-7d	1
c R.J.Langridge								
b N.I.Thomson	3	91					64-3	
416. Surrey v Leicestershire, Kennington Oval, May 15, 17, 18 (Leicestershire won by six wickets)								
c S.Greensword b J.Cotton	0	268					215	
lbw b C.T.Spencer	15	108-5d					162-4	2
417. Surrey v Worcestershire, Kennington Oval, May 19, 20, 21 (Match drawn)								
c R.Booth b L.J.Coldwell	18	216					207	
b N.Gifford	35	169-5					237-7	
418. ENGLAND v NEW ZEALAND, Edgbaston, May 27, 28, 29, 31, June 1 (England won by nine wickets)								
c A.E.Dick b R.O.Collinge	137	435	-	-	-	-		116	
did not bat	-	96-1	5	0	25	0		413	1
419. Surrey v Nottinghamshire, Trent Bridge, June 5, 7, 8 (Match drawn)								
c A.J.Corran b A.A.Johnson	23	279-9d					278-9d	1
								22-2	
420. Surrey v New Zealanders, Kennington Oval, June 9, 10, 11 (Match drawn)								
c G.E.Vivian b V.Pollard	70	248	29	2	88	5	G.T.Dowling c and b	422-9d	2
							A.E.Dick lbw	
							B.R.Taylor c D.Gibson	
							R.W.Morgan c A.Long	
							V.Pollard c R.A.E.Tindall	
not out	129	295-4						
421. Surrey v Oxford University, The Parks, June 12, 14, 15 (Match drawn)								
did not bat	-	175-0d	11	2	27	2	D.P.Toft c and b	161-7d	1
							P.J.K.Gibbs lbw	
did not bat	-	4-0	9	5	13	0		86	
422. Surrey v Gloucestershire, Bristol, June 16, 17, (18) (Match drawn)								
c and b A.R.Windows	7	321-8d					63-2	
423. Surrey v Kent, Kennington Oval, June 19, 21, (22) (Match drawn)								
c B.W.Luckhurst b J.C.J.Dye	5	239					95-1	
424. Surrey v Essex, Kennington Oval, June 26, 28, 29 (Match drawn)								
c and b B.R.Knight	60	320-9d					200	
			23	9	50	1	K.W.R.Fletcher	
							c D.A.D.Sydenham	275-8	

425. Surrey v Northamptonshire, Northampton, June 30, July 1 (Surrey won by an innings and 134 runs)
run out 32 361-9d 78 2
149

426. Surrey v Yorkshire, Bradford, July 3, 4, 6 (Surrey won by three wickets)
c J H Hampshire
  b R.A.Hutton 0 224 147 2
b R.A.Hutton 76 210-7 283-3d

427. ENGLAND v NEW ZEALAND, Headingley, July 8, 9, 10, 12, 13 (England won by an innings and 187 runs)
c J.T.Ward b R.C.Motz 163 546-4d 193
166 2

428. Surrey v Middlesex, Kennington Oval, July 17, 19, 20 (Match drawn)
c R.A.Gale b F.J.Titmus 109 291 6 0 21 0 309-6d
- - - - 185 1

429. ENGLAND v SOUTH AFRICA, Lord's, July 22, 23, 24, 26, 27 (Match drawn)
run out 91 338 280 2
lbw b R.Dumbrill 18 145-7 248 1

430. Surrey v Lancashire, Old Trafford, July (28), (29), 30 (Match drawn)
did not bat - 100-1 96

431. Surrey v Nottinghamshire, Kennington Oval, July 31, August 2, 3 (Match drawn)
c J.B.Bolus b C.Forbes 10 101-5d 3 0 5 0 169
st G.Millman b K.Gillhouley 36 135-8 - - - - 132-4d 1

432. ENGLAND v SOUTH AFRICA, Trent Bridge, August 5, 6, 7, 9 (South Africa won by 94 runs)
b P.M.Pollock 1 240 269
c D.T.Lindsay b P.M.Pollock 1 224 289

433. Surrey v Somerset, Weston-super-Mare, August 11, 12, 13 (Surrey won by eight wickets)
c M.G.M.Groves
  b W.E.Alley 22 226 - - - - 162 3
not out 40 108-2 2 0 2 1 M.G.M.Groves c and b 170 1

434. Surrey v Yorkshire, Kennington Oval, August 14, 16, 17 (Match drawn)
c J.H.Hampshire
  b R.A.Hutton 54 248 11 2 30 2 G.Boycott
                                      c D.A.D.Sydenham 251-5d 1
                                    P.J.Sharpe c and b
c P.J.Sharpe b R.A.Hutton 4 223-7d 11 3 28 2 J.H.Hampshire lbw 175-7 2
                                    R.A.Hutton c and b

435. Surrey v Worcestershire, Worcester, August 21, 23, 24 (Worcestershire won by an innings and 92 runs)
c D.N.F.Slade b L.J.Coldwell 9 94 6 1 23 0 314-8d
c D.N.F.Slade b N.Gifford 3 128

436. ENGLAND v SOUTH AFRICA, Kennington Oval, August 26, 27, 28, 30, 31 (Match drawn)
b J.T.Botten 18 202 208 1
lbw b P.M.Pollock 73 308-4 392 1

437. Surrey v Sussex, Kennington Oval, September 1, 2, (3) (Match drawn)
lbw b N.I.Thomson 5 128 127 3
lbw b J.A.Snow 0 135-4

438. An England XI v A Rest of the World XI, Scarborough, September 8, 9, 10 (Match drawn)
not out 11 160-2d 2.4 0 14 1 C.C.Griffith b 215
- - - - 153-4 1

SEASON'S AVERAGES

Batting and Fielding	M	I	NO	Runs	HS	Ave	100	50	Ct
Test matches	5	8	0	502	163	62.75	2	2	8
Championship	18	28	1	608	109	22.51	1	3	21
Other Surrey matches	4	4	2	263	129	131.50	1	1	6
Other matches	1	1	1	11	11*	-	-	-	1
Season	28	41	4	1384	163	37.40	4	6	36
Career	438	682	109	26211	256	45.74	62	142	433

Bowling	O	M	R	W	BB	Ave	5i
Test matches	5	0	25	0	-	-	-
Championship	69.2	17	186	8	2-9	23.25	-
Other Surrey matches	49	9	128	7	5-88	18.28	1
Other matches	2.4	0	14	1	1-14	14.00	-
Season	126	26	353	16	5-88	22.06	1
Career (6 ball)	1904.1	390 ⎱	6424	196	7-40	32.77	5
Career (8 ball)	121.2	17 ⎰					

1965/66 - MCC in Australia

A slow start for Barrington to the tour was caused by reaction to the news of the death of his father-in-law. He found his form at Melbourne when in a match against Victoria he scored 158. In a shared series, he scored two centuries including the fastest of the year (122 balls in the final Test at Melbourne). With his intense concentration, he was finding touring very tiring and he was allowed to leave the tour before the New Zealand section.

		Own Team Total	O	M	R	W		Opp Total	Ct
439. MCC v Combined XI, Perth, November 5, 6, 8, 9 (Match drawn)									
c M.T.Vernon b L.C.Mayne	3	379-7d						231-5d	
did not bat	-	205-4d						322-6d	
440. MCC v South Australia, Adelaide, November 12, 13, 15, 16 (MCC won by six wickets)									
c B.N.Jarman									
b N.J.N.Hawke	69	310	-	-	-	-		103	1
c D.Robins b D.J.Sincock	51	158-4	3	0	22	0		364	2
441. MCC v Victoria, Melbourne, November 19, 20, 22, 23 (Victoria won by 32 runs)									
c D.R.Cowper									
b K.R.Stackpole	12	211	4	0	9	0		384-7d	
c D.R.Cowper									
b A.N.Connolly	158	306	7	1	24	4	G.D.Watson c M.C.Cowdrey	165	
							P.D.Williams b		
							A.N.Connolly c I.J.Jones		
							R.W.Rayson c J.T.Murray		
442. MCC v Queensland, Brisbane, December 3, 4, 6, 7 (Match drawn)									
not out	80	452-5d						222	2
not out	9	123-2d						315-8d	
443. ENGLAND v AUSTRALIA, Brisbane, December 10, (11), 13, 14, 15 (Match drawn)									
b N.J.N.Hawke	53	280						443-6d	1
c B.C.Booth b R.M.Cowper	38	186-3							
444. MCC v South Australia, Adelaide, December 23, 24, 27, 28 (MCC won by six wickets)									
st B.N.Jarman b D.J.Sincock	63	444	1	0	5	0		459-7d	
did not bat	-	270-4	-	-	-	-		253-4d	
445. ENGLAND v AUSTRALIA, Melbourne, December 30, 31, January 1, 3, 4 (Match drawn)									
c P.J.P.Burge b T.R.Veivers	63	558	-	-	-	-		358	
did not bat	-	5-0	7.4	0	47	2	K.D.Walters c and b	426	2
							A.T.W.Grout c D.A.Allen		
446. ENGLAND v AUSTRALIA, Sydney, January 7, 8, 10, 11 (England won by an innings and 93 runs)									
c G.D.McKenzie									
b N.J.N.Hawke	1	488						221	
								174	
447. MCC v Combined XI, Hobart, January 22, 24, 25 (Match drawn)									
c L.V.Maddocks b K.Hooper	37	471-9d	-	-	-	-		199	2
			10	0	42	0		273-1	
448. ENGLAND v AUSTRALIA, Adelaide, January 28, 29, 31, February 1 (Australia won by an innings and 9 runs)									
lbw b K.D.Walters	60	241						516	
c I.M.Chappell									
b N.J.N.Hawke	102	266							

449. ENGLAND v AUSTRALIA, Melbourne, February 11, 12, 14, (15), 16 (Match drawn)
    c A.T.W.Grout
         b K.D.Walters   115   485-9d   543-8d
    not out   32   69-3

SEASON'S AVERAGES

Batting and Fielding	M	I	NO	Runs	HS	Ave	100	50	Ct
Test matches	5	8	1	464	115	66.28	2	3	3
Other matches	6	9	2	482	158	68.85	1	4	9
Season	11	17	3	946	158	67.57	3	7	10
Career	449	699	112	27157	256	46.26	65	149	443

Bowling	O	M	R	W	BB	Ave	5i
Test matches	7.4	0	47	2	2-47	23.50	-
Other matches	25	1	102	4	4-24	25.50	-
Season	32.4	1	149	6	4-24	24.83	-
Career (6 ball)	1904.1	390 }	6573	202	7-40	32.53	5
Career (8 ball)	153.6	18 }					

1966

Barrington found that he lacked a sense of anticipation when the first ball of the season came to be bowled. At the end of May, however, he scored centuries against Northamptonshire and Nottinghamshire. England lost the First Test, Barrington finding Griffith difficult to handle. Unknown to friend and foe alike, he was suffering an acute mental and physical breakdown. His doctor recommended an immediate holiday, but he continued playing and had a bad match at Lord's. He then took a holiday at Bournemouth and returned to the Surrey team at the end of July, scored a century against Lancashire and still finished fourth overall in the national averages. During this season, the first innings of some County Championship matches was restricted to 65 overs.

	Own Team Total	O	M	R	W		Opp Total	Ct
450. Surrey v MCC, Lord's, May 4, 5, (6) (Match drawn)								
							192-3d	
451. Surrey v Derbyshire, Kennington Oval, May 7, 9, 10 (Derbyshire won by 7 runs)								
b E.Smith	0 97	8	0	21	0		136	2
c J.F.Harvey b E.Smith	48 117	-	-	-	-		85	1
452. Surrey v Sussex, Kennington Oval, May 11, 12, 13 (Surrey won by nine wickets)								
c Nawab of Pataudi								
b D.L.Bates	41 216-7						155-6	
did not bat	- 42-1						102	
453. Surrey v Glamorgan, Kennington Oval, May 14, 16, 17 (Match drawn)								
run out	2 80	-	-	-	-		131	1
c A.Rees b F.J.Davis	10 246-7	9	3	6	1	W.D.Slade lbw	252	
454. Surrey v Hampshire, Basingstoke, May 18, 19, 20 (Match drawn)								
lbw b D.Shackleton	8 143-8d	-	-	-	-		259-6d	1
c D.Shackleton								
b P.J.Sainsbury	22 83-6	5	1	18	0		62-1d	
455. Surrey v Northamptonshire, Kennington Oval, May (25), 26, 27 (Match drawn)								
not out	103 157-9d						207-6d	
ç C.Milburn b B.S.Crump	1 181-7						181-3d	
456. Surrey v Nottinghamshire, Trent Bridge, May 28, 30, 31 (Match drawn)								
not out	49 239-4c	-	-	-	-		233-8c	
c A.A.Johnson								
b R.A.White	106 331-5d	22	7	45	3	R.Swetman c and b H.I.Moore c and b J.M.Parkin c A.Long	261-7	3

457. ENGLAND v WEST INDIES, Old Trafford, June 2, 3, 4 (West Indies won by an innings and 40 runs)
c and b C.C.Griffith   5   167   484
c S.M.Nurse
     b D.A.J.Holford   30   277

458. Surrey v Kent, Kennington Oval, June 11, 12, 13 (Match drawn)
c A.G.E.Ealham
     b D.L.Underwood   7   156-9c   -   -   -   -   179-8c
c J.C.J.Dye b A.Brown   68   229   1   0   1   0   168-9

459. ENGLAND v WEST INDIES, Lord's, June 16, 17, 18, 20, 21 (Match drawn)
b G.St A.Sobers   19   355   269
b C.C.Griffith   5   197-4   369-5d

460. Surrey v Leicestershire, Leicester, June 25, 26, (27) (Match drawn)
c G.A.R.Lock b P.T.Marner   2   81   195-8c
     23-2

461. Surrey v Essex, Kennington Oval, July 30, 31, August 1 (Surrey won by seven wickets)
b B.R.Knight   19   92-3d   141-5d
not out   13   165-3   115-6d

462. Surrey v Nottinghamshire, Kennington Oval, August 3, 4, 5 (Match drawn)
c R.Swetman
     b M.N.S.Taylor   36   283-7d   -   -   -   -   116   1
     7   2   27   1   C.Forbes   c M.J.Stewart   352-8   1

463. Surrey v Middlesex, Lord's, August 6, 8, 9 (Match drawn)
c R.W.Hooker b R.W.Stewart 0   200-5c   95
c R.W.Stewart
     b R.W.Hooker   20   123-9d   57-1

464. Surrey v Yorkshire, Bradford, August 13, 15, 16 (Surrey won by 21 runs)
b D.B.Close   33   189-9c   115   1
b R.Illingworth   4   98   151

465. Surrey v Gloucestershire, Cheltenham, August 17, 18 (Surrey won by seven wickets)
c B.J.Meyer b D.R.Smith   76   200-6c   -   -   -   -   119
not out   9   109-3   2   1   4   0   189

466. Surrey v Sussex, Eastbourne, August 20, 22, 23 (Match drawn)
c K.G.Suttle b D.L.Bates   27   279-4d   15   4   34   2   K.G.Suttle   c A.Long   237
                                                       J.M.Parks   b
b A.Buss   50   221-8   10   0   39   0   275-7d   1

467. Surrey v Gloucestershire, Kennington Oval, August 24, 25, 26 (Match drawn)
lbw b D.R.Smith   0   321-6d   -   -   -   -   258   2
not out   57   158-3d   13   0   87   3   M.Bissex   lbw   220-9   1
                                       S.E.J.Russell   c M.J.Edwards
                                       D.R.Shepherd   c R.I.Jefferson

468. Surrey v Yorkshire, Kennington Oval, August 27, 29, (30) (Match drawn)
c P.J.Sharpe b D.B.Close   0   150   143   2
     108-5   1

469. Surrey v Lancashire, Old Trafford, August 31, September 2, (3) (Match drawn)
not out   117   234-9d   112-6

SEASON'S AVERAGES

Batting and Fielding	M	I	NO	Runs	HS	Ave	100	50	Ct
Test matches	2	4	0	59	30	14.75	-	-	-
Championship	17	29	6	928	117*	40.34	3	4	18
Other Surrey matches	1	0							
Season	20	33	6	987	117*	36.55	3	4	18
Career	469	732	118	28144	256	45.83	68	153	461

Bowling	O	M	R	W	BB	Ave	5i
Championship	92	18	282	10	3-45	28.20	-
Career (6 ball)	1996.1	408 }	6855	212	7-40	32.33	5
Career (8 ball)	153.6	18 }					

1967

There was no tour in the winter and Barrington played golf and restricted acceptance of invitations to only small social gatherings. In May he hit six half-centuries in seven innings and captained Surrey to an eight wicket victory over the Indian touring team. In the three match series against India, all matches were won and Barrington scored three fifties. For Surrey against Yorkshire he scored 158 and took 5 for 51, his best ever Championship bowling figures. There were two wins against Pakistan with Barrington scoring two centuries and becoming the sixth batsman to pass 6,000 runs in Test cricket.

	Own Team Total	O	M	R	W		Opp Total	Ct
470. Surrey v Oxford University, The Parks, April 29, May 1, 2 (Match drawn)								
c F.S.Goldstein								
b A.H.Barker	26 316-5d	10	3	27	3	D.A.Ashworth c J.H.Edrich	198	1
						G.N.S.Ridley c and b		
						N.W.Gamble b		
		13	2	30	0		173-9	
471. Surrey v MCC, Lord's, May 3, (4), (5) (Match drawn)								
st J.H.Murray								
b R.N.S.Hobbs	62 266						36-3	
472. Surrey v Warwickshire, Kennington Oval, May 6, 8, 9 (Match drawn)								
not out	63 175-6d						224-2d	
c R.W.Barber								
b R.B.Edmonds	95 227-8						205-5d	
473. Surrey v Hampshire, Kennington Oval, May 10, 11, 12 (Hampshire won by an innings and 15 runs)								
b R.M.H.Cottam	41 123	3	0	20	0		329-7d	1
c M.J.Horton								
b R.M.H.Cottam	60 191							
474. Surrey v Northamptonshire, Northampton, May (17), 18, (19) (Match drawn)								
c D.S.Steele b M.K.Kettle	82 356-8d						8-0	
475. Surrey v Derbyshire, Chesterfield, May (20), 21, (22) (Match drawn)								
							69-1	
476. Surrey v Warwickshire, Nuneaton, May (24), 25, (26) (Match drawn)								
							180-9	
477. Surrey v Essex, Kennington Oval, May (27), (28), 29 (Match drawn)								
c B.E.A.Edmeades								
b R.N.S.Hobbs	14 213-4d	8	1	48	2	B.E.A.Edmeades c and b	188-8	1
						K.D.Boyce c G.G.Arnold		
478. Surrey v Indians, Kennington Oval, May 31, June 1, 2 (Surrey won by eight wickets)								
b S.Guha	84 313-9d	-	-	- -			161	
not out	27 74-2	6	0	27	0		225	2
479. Surrey v Leicestershire, Guildford, June 3, 4, 5 (Surrey won by ten wickets)								
c R.W.Tolchard								
b G.A.R.Lock	32 252	-	-	- -			93	
did not bat	- 28-0	5	1	11	0		186	1
480. ENGLAND v INDIA, Headingley, June 8, 9, 10, 12, 13 (England won by six wickets)								
run out	93 550-4d	-	-	- -			164	1
c F.M.Engineer								
b B.S.Chandrasekhar	46 126-4	9	1	38	0		510	
481. Surrey v Worcestershire, Kennington Oval, June 17, 19, 20 (Surrey won by an innings and 117 runs)								
not out	142 401-5d						207	
							77	
482. ENGLAND v INDIA, Lord's, June 22, 23, 24, 26 (England won by an innings and 124 runs)								
b B.S.Chandrasekhar	97 386						132	
							110	
483. Surrey v Kent, Kennington Oval, June 28, 29, 30 (Kent won by 72 runs)								
c J.N.Shepherd b J.N.Graham 0	132						220	1
lbw b D.L.Underwood	5 177						161-8d	

484. Surrey v Glamorgan, Kennington Oval, July 1, 2, 3 (Glamorgan won by four wickets)
c P.M.Walker b R.C.Davis 14 312 10 2 31 1 A.Jones c G.G.Arnold 246-8d
did not bat - 160-0d 10 1 39 3 A.Jones lbw 227-6
                                      A.Rees b
                                      E.A.Cordle c sub

485. Surrey v Lancashire, Old Trafford, July 5, 6, 7 (Match drawn)
c K.Goodwin b K.Higgs 20 200 - - - - 185
not out 33 96-3 5 0 14 0 266-4d

486. Surrey v Middlesex, Kennington Oval, July 8, 9, 10 (Match drawn)
c W.E.Russell b P.H.Parfitt 113 372-3d 6 2 19 1 R.W.Stewart lbw 277
lbw b F.J.Titmus 10 133 10 1 15 0 138-5 2

487. ENGLAND v INDIA, Edgbaston, July 13, 14, 15 (England won by 132 runs)
c A.L.Wadekar
   b E.A.S.Prasanna 75 298 92
c B.K.Kunderan
   c B.S.Chandrasekhar 13 203 277 1

488. Surrey v Northamptonshire, Kennington Oval, July 19, 20, 21 (Surrey won by an innings and 83 runs)
b H.Sully 13 368 - - - - 101 2
  7 2 18 2 Mushtaq Mohammed
             c S.J.Storey 184 2
           M.K.Kettle c and b

489. Surrey v Yorkshire, Kennington Oval, July 22, 24, 25 (Surrey won by an innings and 8 runs)
not out 158 395-8d 20.2 5 51 5 P.J.Sharpe c S.J.Storey 178 2
                              D.E.V.Padgett b
                              K.Taylor c and b
                              R.Illingworth b
                              F.S.Trueman c G.G.Arnold
  25 7 54 2 D.E.V.Padgett
              c Younis Ahmed 209 1
            J.H.Hampshire c and b

490. ENGLAND v PAKISTAN, Lord's, July 27, 28, 29, 31, August 1 (Match drawn)
c Wasim Bari
   b Asif Iqbal Razvi 148 369 11 1 29 1 Wasim Bari c D.B.Close 354 1
b Intikhab Alam Khan 14 241-9d 13 2 23 2 Javed Burki c and b 88-3 1
                              Majid Khan c D.B.Close

491. Surrey v Gloucestershire, Kennington Oval, August 5, 6, 7 (Surrey won by seven wickets)
c C.A.Milton b M.Bissex 20 259 10 1 23 0 351
c A.S.Brown
   b J.B.Mortimore 36 206-3 6 2 16 0 113

492. ENGLAND v PAKISTAN, Trent Bridge, August 10, 11, 12, (14), 15 (England won by ten wickets)
not out 109 252-8d 140
did not bat - 3-0 114 1

493. Surrey v Middlesex, Lord's, August (19), 20, 21 (Match drawn)
c J.T.Murray b R.S.Herman 0 294-8 194 2

494. ENGLAND v PAKISTAN, Kennington Oval, August 24, 25, 26, 28 (England won by eight wickets)
c Wasim Bari
   b Saleem Altaf Bokhari 142 440 - - - - 216
not out 13 34-2 8 2 29 0 255

495. Surrey v Nottinghamshire, Kennington Oval, August 30, 31, September 1 (Match drawn)
not out 59 364-9d 11 4 28 0 290-8d 1
not out 48 134-5d - - - - 14-0

496. T.N.Pearce's XI v Pakistanis, Scarborough, September 2, 4, 5 (Match drawn)
not out 29 310-7d 8 0 41 0 365-7d
c Saeed Ahmed b Arif Butt 2 144-6 - - - - 141-9d

497. An England XI v Rest of World XI, Scarborough, September 6, 7, 8 (Match drawn)
b L.R.Gibbs 8 201 5 0 31 1 K.C.Bland st J.T.Murray 355-6d
c P.M.Pollock b L.R.Gibbs 13 291-6 2 0 21 0 238-2d

SEASON'S AVERAGES

Batting and Fielding	M	I	NO	Runs	HS	Ave	100	50	Ct
Test matches	6	10	2	750	148	93.75	3	3	5
Championship	17	22	6	1058	158*	66.12	3	5	16
Other Surrey matches	3	4	1	199	84	66.33	-	2	3
Other matches	2	4	1	52	29	17.33	-	-	-
Season	28	40	10	2059	158*	68.63	6	10	24
Career	497	772	128	30203	256	46.89	74	163	485

Bowling	O	M	R	W	BB	Ave	5i
Test matches	41	6	119	3	2-23	39.66	-
Championship	136.2	29	387	16	5-51	24.18	1
Other Surrey matches	29	5	84	3	3-27	28.00	-
Other matches	15	0	93	1	1-31	93.00	-
Season	221.2	40	683	23	5-51	29.69	1
Career (6 ball)	2217.3	448 }	7538	235	7-40	32.07	6
Career (8 ball)	153.6	18 }					

1967/68 - MCC in the West Indies

Barrington said that this was going to be his last tour. In the First Test he had a battle with Griffith, who bowled with great hostility, and came out on top scoring 143 in a drawn match. It was a very tiring tour with constant taunts from the crowds but England triumphed in the end winning the Second Test at Port-of-Spain, although many blamed Sobers for his over generous declaration.

	Own	Team Total	O	M	R	W		Opp Total	Ct
498. MCC v President's XI, Bridgetown, January 3, 4, 5, 6 (Match drawn)									
run out	1	365	27	4	99	5	R.C.Fredericks c G.Boycott	435-9d	2
							M.L.C.Foster c and b		
							D.L.Murray c and b		
							W.English c J.M.Parks		
							R.M.Edwards c M.C.Cowdrey		
not out	53	94-2	4	0	30	0		116-1d	
499. MCC v Trinidad, Port of Spain, January 9, 10, 11, 12 (Match drawn)									
c R.DeSousa									
b W.V.Rodriguez	1	207	21.1	2	52	1	R.DeSouza c and b	321	1
c A.Clarke b W.W.Hall	17	188-6	7	0	27	0		204-3d	1
500. ENGLAND v WEST INDIES, Port of Spain, January 19, 20, 22, 23, 24 (Match drawn)									
c C.C.Griffith b L.R.Gibbs	143	568	18	6	44	1	G.St A.Sobers		
							c T.W.Graveney	363	
			15	0	69	1	G.S.Camacho		
							c T.W.Graveney	243-8	
501. MCC v Jamaica, Kingston, January 31, February 1, 2, 3 (MCC won by 174 runs)									
c L.A.King b L.Wellington	6	135	1	0	6	0		98	
lbw b L.A.King	32	343-6d	11	4	34	2	O.Miles c T.W.Graveney	206	
							C.Folkes c M.C.Cowdrey		
502. ENGLAND v WEST INDIES, Kingston, February 8, 9, 10, 12, 13, 14 (Match drawn)									
c and b D.A.J.Holford	63	376	-	-	-	-		143	
lbw b C.C.Griffith	13	68-8	6	1	14	0		391-9d	
503. MCC v Leeward Islands, Antigua, February 15, 16, 17 (Match drawn)									
not out	100	362-1d	12.5	1	35	0		141	
did not bat	-	8-0	10	1	40	0		323-8d	
504. MCC v Barbados, Bridgetown, February 22, 23, 24, 26 (Match drawn)									
not out	69	578-5d	6	1	23	0		276	
			12	3	27	0		161-5	
505. ENGLAND v WEST INDIES, Bridgetown, February 29, March 1, 2, 4, 5 (Match drawn)									
c B.F.Butcher b W.W.Hall	17	449	8	1	29	1	G.S.Camacho		
							c T.W.Graveney	349	1
			4	0	17	0		284-6	

509–506 match records:

506. MCC v Windward Islands, Castries, March 8, 9, (11) (Match drawn)
c C.Charlemangne
b K.Laurent   24 215   2   0   6   0   165
did not bat   - 34-3

507. ENGLAND v WEST INDIES, Port of Spain, March 14, 15, 16, 18, 19 (England won by seven wickets)
lbw b L.R.Gibbs   48 404   10   2 41   1 S.M.Nurse c J.H.Edrich   526-7d   1
did not bat   - 215-3   -   -   -   -   92-2d

508. ENGLAND v WEST INDIES, Georgetown, March 28, 29, 30, April 1, 2, 3 (Match drawn)
c R.B.Kanhai b G.St A.Sobers 4 371 18   4 43   1 G.St A.Sobers
                                                     c M.C.Cowdrey   414
c C.H.Lloyd b L.R.Gibbs   0 206-9 -   -   -   -   264

SEASON'S AVERAGES

Batting and Fielding	M	I	NO	Runs	HS	Ave	100	50	Ct
Test matches	5	7	0	288	143	41.14	1	1	2
Other matches	6	9	3	303	100*	50.50	1	2	4
Season	11	16	3	591	143	45.46	2	3	6
Career	508	788	131	30794	256	46.87	76	166	491

Bowling	O	M	R	W	BB	Ave	5i
Test matches	79	14	257	5	1-29	51.40	-
Other matches	114	19	379	8	5-99	47.37	1
Season	193	33	636	13	5-99	48.92	1
Career (6 ball)	2410.3	481 }	8174	248	7-40	32.95	7
Career (8 ball)	153.6	18 }					

1968

During May, Barrington was laid low with gastric flu and was out of cricket for ten days, coming back to make a pair against Derbyshire. He was picked for the First Test but withdrew with back problems. At Lord's he scored 75 in a match ruined by rain when England were in a strong position. A duck at Edgbaston followed by 49 and 46 not out at Headingley and he was then dropped for the Oval match. Barrington had a disappointing end to his last first-class season when scoring only 30 runs in six innings.

	Own	Team Total	O	M	R	W		Opp Total	Ct

509. Surrey v MCC, Lord's, May 1, 2, 3 (Match drawn)
c K.W.R.Fletcher
b K.Shuttleworth   24 257-8d   -   -   -   -   185   1
st R.W.Tolchard
b D.A.Allen   25 130   1   0   8   0   163-7

510. Surrey v Northamptonshire, Kennington Oval, May 4, 6, 7 (Surrey won by eight wickets)
absent ill   - 191   87
                    - 51-2   154

511. Surrey v Derbyshire, Kennington Oval, May 15, 16, 17 (Match drawn)
lbw b H.J.Rhodes   0 85   150
b H.J.Rhodes   0 165-7   190-5d 1

512. Surrey v Oxford University, The Parks, May 18, 20, 21 (Surrey won by ten wickets)
lbw b A.J.Khan   30 157   50
did not bat   - 38-0   141

513. Surrey v Essex, Romford, May 22, 23, 24 (Surrey won by eight wickets)
c B.Taylor b R.N.S.Hobbs 41 207   -   -   -   -   138-9d 1
not out   6 75-2 5.4 3   6   1 R.E.East b   141

514. Surrey v Warwickshire, Edgbaston, May 29, 30, 31 (Warwickshire won by eight wickets)
b J.D.Bannister   4 245 26   7 57   4 K.Ibadulla c M.J.Stewart   249   1
                                                  J.A.Jameson c J.H.Edrich
                                                  A.Gordon c M.J.Edwards
                                                  J.D.Bannister c A.Long
c R.N.Abberley b L.R.Gibbs 5 117   4   0 23   0   116-2

515. Surrey v Leicestershire, Kennington Oval, June 12, 13, 14 (Match drawn)
c D.J.Constant
    b J.Birkenshaw 1 204   12 2 51 1 P.T.Marner c A.Long   392-8d 2
c C.C.Inman b J.Birkenshaw 25 314-5

516. Surrey v Essex, Guildford, June 15, 16, 17 (Match drawn)
b S.Turner   11 251-8d 8 0 58 0   376 1
b S.Turner   52 148-4   7 2 23 0   156-5d 1

517. ENGLAND v AUSTRALIA, Lord's, June 20, 21, 22, 24, 25 (Match drawn)
c B.N.Jarman
    b A.N.Connolly 75 351-7d - - - -   78
                            2 0 12 1 R.M.Cowper
                                                c D.L.Underwood 127-4

518. Surrey v Somerset, Kennington Oval, June 26, 27, 28 (Match drawn)
b G.S.Chappell 44 210-9d   116 1
did not bat - 19-0

519. Surrey v Middlesex, Lord's, June 29, 30, July 1 (Middlesex won by seven wickets)
c and b P.H.Parfitt 3 103 3.3 1 5 2 R.W.Hooker b   122
                                          R.S.Herman b
c R.W.Hooker b F.J.Titmus 0 206 18.5 5 42 0   191-3 1

520. Surrey v Sussex, Kennington Oval, July 6, 7, 8 (Match drawn)
not out 29 200-3d 18 8 26 1 G.C.Cooper lbw   201 2
c G.C.Cooper b E.J.Lewis 11 100-6 29 5 64 2 A.S.M.Oakman
                                              c G.R.J.Roope 165-8d
                                  J.M.Parks c G.R.J.Roope

521. ENGLAND v AUSTRALIA, Edgbaston, July (11), 12, 13, 15, 16 (Match drawn)
lbw b E.W.Freeman 0 409   222 1
did not bat - 142-3d   68-1

522. Surrey v Nottinghamshire, Kennington Oval, July 17, 18, 19 (Match drawn)
c G.St A.Sobers
    b R.A.White 16 163-9d - - - -   124
b M.N.S.Taylor 43 216-7d 10 2 24 3 J.M.Parkin c M.J.Stewart 230-9
                                          D.L.Murray lbw
                                          D.J.Halfyard c J.H.Edrich

523. Surrey v Yorkshire, Kennington Oval, July 20, 21, 22 (Yorkshire won by an innings and 32 runs)
b R.Illingworth 37 105 13 2 35 1 K.Taylor lbw   320
c and b D.Wilson 11 183

524. ENGLAND v AUSTRALIA, Headingley, July 25, 26, 27, 29, 30 (Match drawn)
b A.N.Connolly 49 302 - - - -   315 1
not out 46 230-4 6 1 14 0   312 1

525. Surrey v Gloucestershire, Kennington Oval, August 3, 4, 5 (Match drawn)
b D.M.Green 13 312 - - - -   120
                      26 9 42 1 D.M.Green c J.H.Edrich 293-2

526. Surrey v Nottinghamshire, Trent Bridge, August 10, 11, 12 (Match drawn)
c M.N.S.Taylor
    b G.St A.Sobers 29 203 11 1 49 0   313-8d 1
lbw b C.Forbes 63 262-8 - - - -   163-7d 1

527. Surrey v Kent, Kennington Oval, August 14, 15, 16 (Match drawn)
lbw b J.N.Shepherd 4 190   300 1
not out 5 42-2

528. Surrey v Gloucestershire, Cheltenham, August 17, 18, 19 (Match drawn)
c A.S.Brown b D.A.Allen 21 176 17.2 4 47 5 M.Bissex c and b   242 1
                                            J.Sullivan lbw
                                        D.A.Allen c M.J.Edwards
                                          B.J.Meyer c R.D.Jackman
                                          D.R.Smith c R.Harman
c M.J.Proctor b M.Bissex 1 43-6 - - - -   104-4d

529. Surrey v Glamorgan, Neath, August 21, 22 (Glamorgan won by ten wickets)
b D.J.Shepherd 17 86 4.4 1 20 2 Majid Jahangir c R.Harman 210
                                          O.S.Wheatley c P.I.Pocock
b B.Lewis 24 174 6 1 15 0   51-0

530. Surrey v Northamptonshire, Northampton, August 24, 25, 26 (Northamptonshire won by three wickets)
b H.Sully 71 241 13 5 28 1 A.Lightfoot b   228-9d 2
not out 54 240-5d 5 0 31 0   257-7

531. Surrey v Yorkshire, Hull, August 28, 29, 30 (Yorkshire won by 60 runs)
    c R.A.Hutton

b R.Illingworth	10	189	327-9d	1
c A.G.Nicholson b D.Wilson	9	190	112-7d	

532. Surrey v Worcestershire, Worcester, August 31, September 2, 3 (Match drawn)

b L.J.Coldwell	2	209-8d	-	-	-	-	114
c A.R.P.Barker b N.Gifford	1	75-8	21	6	53	0	275-5d

533. Surrey v Hampshire, Kennington Oval, September 4, 5, 6 (Match drawn)

run out	0	227-4d	175-6d	1
c R.M.C.Gilliat				
b D.A.Livingstone	8	134-4d	133-8	

SEASON'S AVERAGES

Batting and Fielding	M	I	NO	Runs	HS	Ave	100	50	Ct
Test matches	3	4	1	170	75	56.66	-	1	3
Championship	20	36	4	671	71	20.96	-	4	19
Other Surrey matches	2	3	0	79	30	26.33	-	-	1
Season	25	43	5	920	75	24.21	-	5	23
Career	533	831	136	31714	256	45.63	76	171	514

Bowling	O	M	R	W	BB	Ave	5i
Test matches	8	1	26	1	1-12	26.00	-
Championship	259	64	699	24	5-47	29.12	1
Other Surrey matches	1	0	8	0	-	-	-
Season	268	65	733	25	5-47	29.32	1
Career (6 ball)	2678.3	546 }	8907	273	7-40	32.62	8
Career (8 ball)	153.6	18 }					

Season by Season Record (Batting and Fielding)

Season		M	I	NO	R	HS	Ave	100	50	Ct
1953		9	14	1	237	81	18.23	-	1	4
1954		19	25	4	845	108*	40.23	3	3	16
1955		35	55	7	1580	135*	32.91	2	9	21
1955/56	Pakistan	12	17	2	586	87	39.06	-	5	6
1956		31	54	10	1323	109*	30.06	2	6	20
1957		35	53	11	1642	136	39.09	6	7	64
1958		34	45	9	1147	101*	31.86	1	6	55
1959		32	52	6	2499	186	54.32	6	13	45
1959/60	Rhodesia	2	4	0	165	111	41.25	1	-	3
1959/60	West Indies	12	19	1	830	128	46.11	3	4	7
1960		31	53	9	1878	126	42.68	2	16	22
1960/61	South Africa	4	7	0	164	66	23.42	-	1	3
1961		24	42	7	2070	163	59.14	4	15	31
1961/62	India, Pakistan, Ceylon	17	26	7	1329	172	69.94	5	6	12
1962		29	46	8	1865	146	49.07	6	9	24
1962/63	Australia	13	22	5	1451	219*	85.35	5	7	12
1962/63	New Zealand	4	5	0	312	126	62.40	1	1	5
1963		28	45	7	1568	110*	41.26	2	11	18
1963/64	India	4	4	1	336	108	112.00	1	3	2
1964		22	35	5	1872	256	62.40	4	9	20
1964/65	South Africa	13	18	5	1128	169*	86.76	4	4	7
1965		28	41	4	1384	163	37.40	4	6	36
1965/66	Australia	11	17	3	946	158	67.57	3	7	10
1966		20	33	6	987	117*	36.55	3	4	18
1967		28	40	10	2059	158*	68.63	6	10	24
1967/68	West Indies	11	16	3	591	143	45.46	2	3	6
1968		25	43	5	920	75	24.21	-	5	23
Total		**533**	**831**	**136**	**31714**	**256**	**45.63**	**76**	**171**	**514**

Season by Season Record (Bowling)

Season		O	M	R	W	BB	Ave	5i
1954		13	2	63	1	1-45	63.00	-
1955		34.3	0	185	7	6-70	26.42	1
1955/56	Pakistan	28.1	9	69	2	1-30	34.50	-
1956		29.3	3	111	2	2-38	55.50	-
1957		36	6	127	4	2-34	31.75	-
1958		155	34	444	15	4-27	29.60	-
1959		227	34	691	20	4-59	34.55	-
1959/60	Rhodesia	46	8	131	5	3-48	26.20	-
1959/60	West Indies	237.4	64	619	17	3-42	36.41	-
1960		190.4	30	710	7	2-67	101.42	-
1960/61	South Africa	58	6	200	7	4-42	28.57	-
1961		161	28	556	9	2-32	61.77	-
1961/62	Ind, Pak, Ceylon	112	27	323	9	2-30	35.88	-
1962		79.3	11	348	6	2-25	58.00	-
1962/63	Australia (8 ball)	121.2	17	523	10	3-55	52.30	-
1962/63	New Zealand	40.3	10	130	7	3-32	18.57	-
1963		77	26	167	9	4-40	18.55	-
1963/64	India	39.5	9	131	7	3-11	18.71	-
1964		139.4	34	369	12	5-46	30.75	1
1964/65	South Africa	73.1	23	174	24	7-40	7.25	2
1965		126	26	353	16	5-88	22.06	1
1965/66	Australia (8 ball)	32.4	1	149	6	4-24	24.83	-
1966		92	18	282	10	3-45	28.20	-
1967		221.2	40	683	23	5-51	29.69	1
1967/68	West Indies	193	33	636	13	5-59	48.92	1
1968		268	65	733	25	5-74	29.32	1
Total	**(6-ball)**	**2546.3**	**546**	**8907**	**273**	**7-40**	**32.62**	**8**
	(8-ball)	**153.6**	**18**					

For England Season by Season (Batting and Fielding)

Season		M	I	NO	R	HS	Ave	100	50	Ct
1955		2	3	0	52	34	17.33	-	-	-
1959		5	6	0	357	87	59.50	-	4	5
1959/60	West Indies	5	9	0	420	128	46.66	2	1	2
1960		4	7	1	227	80	37.83	-	2	-
1961		5	9	1	364	83	45.50	-	4	4
1961/62	India	5	9	3	594	172	99.00	3	1	2
1961/62	Pakistan	2	3	0	229	139	76.33	1	1	1
1962		4	4	1	60	50*	20.00	-	1	3
1962/63	Australia	5	10	2	582	132*	72.75	2	3	6
1962/63	New Zealand	3	4	0	294	126	73.50	1	1	5
1963		5	10	0	275	80	27.50	-	2	3
1963/64	India	1	1	0	80	80	80.00	-	1	-
1964		5	8	1	531	256	75.85	1	2	3
1964/65	South Africa	5	7	2	508	148	101.60	2	2	3
1965	New Zealand	2	2	0	300	163	150.00	2	-	3
1965	South Africa	3	6	0	202	91	33.66	-	2	5
1965/66	Australia	5	8	1	464	115	66.28	2	3	3
1966		2	4	0	59	30	14.75	-	-	-
1967	India	3	5	0	324	97	64.80	-	3	2
1967	Pakistan	3	5	2	426	148	142.00	3	-	3
1967/68	West Indies	5	7	0	288	143	41.14	1	1	2
1968		3	4	1	170	75	56.66	-	1	3
Total		**82**	**131**	**15**	**6806**	**256**	**58.67**	**20**	**35**	**58**

For England Season by Season (Bowling)

Season		O	M	R	W	BB	Ave	5i
1959		47	7	135	5	3-36	27.00	-
1959/60	West Indies	106.5	41	217	5	2-34	43.40	-
1960		3	1	5	0	-	-	-
1961/62	India	12	1	57	0	-	-	-
1961/62	Pakistan	38	14	81	0	-	-	-
1962		6	2	22	0	-	-	-
1962/63	Australia (8 ball)	39	6	154	1	1-44	154.00	-
1962/63	New Zealand	30.3	8	89	4	3-32	22.25	-
1963/64	India	6	0	29	0	-	-	-
1964		1	0	4	0	-	-	-
1964/65	South Africa	7.1	1	33	3	3-4	11.00	-
1965	New Zealand	5	0	25	0	-	-	-
1965/66	Australia (8 ball)	7.4	0	47	2	2-47	23.50	-
1967	India	9	1	38	0	-	-	-
1967	Pakistan	32	5	81	3	2-23	27.00	-
1967/68	West Indies	79	14	257	5	1-29	51.40	-
1968		8	1	26	1	1-12	26.00	-
Total	**(6-ball)**	**390.5**	**96** }	**1300**	**29**	**3-4**	**44.82**	-
	(8-ball)	**46.4**	**6**					

For England Against Each Country (Batting and Fielding)

	M	I	NO	R	HS	Ave	100	50	Ct
Australia	23	39	6	2111	256	63.97	5	13	19
India	14	21	3	1355	172	75.27	3	9	9
New Zealand	5	6	0	594	163	99.00	3	1	8
Pakistan	9	12	3	715	148	79.44	4	2	7
South Africa	14	23	3	989	148	49.45	2	6	8
West Indies	17	30	0	1042	143	34.73	3	4	7
Total	**82**	**131**	**15**	**6806**	**256**	**58.67**	**20**	**35**	**58**

For England Against Each Country (Bowling)

		O	M	R	W	BB	Ave	5i
Australia	(6-ball)	9	1 }	231	4	2-47	57.75	-
	(8-ball)	46.4	6					
India		74	9	259	5	3-36	51.80	-
New Zealand		35.3	8	114	4	3-32	28.50	-
Pakistan		76	21	184	3	2-23	61.33	-
South Africa		10.1	2	38	3	3-4	12.66	-
West Indies		185.5	55	474	10	2-34	47.40	-
Total	**(6-ball)**	**390.5**	**96** }	**1300**	**29**	**3-4**	**44.82**	-
	(8-ball)	**46.4**	**6**					

For Surrey Season by Season (Batting and Fielding)

Season		M	I	NO	R	HS	Ave	100	50	Ct
1953		9	14	1	237	81	18.23	-	1	4
1954		19	25	4	845	108*	40.23	3	3	16
1955		30	46	7	1418	135*	36.35	2	8	15
1956		30	52	9	1250	109*	29.07	2	5	20
1957		35	53	11	1642	136	39.09	6	7	64
1958		32	41	9	926	101*	28.93	1	4	54
1959		23	40	6	1993	186	58.61	6	9	31
1959/60	Rhodesia	2	4	0	165	111	41.25	1	-	3
1960		22	37	8	1323	126	45.62	1	13	17
1961		17	29	6	1510	163	65.65	4	8	25
1962		22	37	7	1472	146	49.06	4	7	17
1963		22	33	7	1269	110*	48.80	2	9	15
1964		17	27	4	1341	207	58.30	3	7	17
1965		22	32	3	871	129*	30.03	2	4	27
1966		18	29	6	928	117*	40.34	3	4	18
1967		20	26	7	1257	158*	66.15	3	7	19
1968		22	39	4	750	71	21.42	-	4	20
Total		**362**	**564**	**99**	**19197**	**207**	**41.28**	**43**	**100**	**382**

For Surrey Season by Season (Bowling)

Season		O	M	R	W	BB	Ave	5i
1954		13	2	63	1	1-45	63.00	-
1955		13.5	0	73	0	-	-	-
1956		29.3	3	111	2	2-38	55.00	-
1957		36	6	127	4	2-34	31.75	-
1958		144	31	395	15	4-27	26.33	-
1959		119	17	357	4	1-22	89.25	-
1959/60	Rhodesia	46	8	131	5	3-48	26.20	-
1960		137.4	24	440	2	1-47	220.00	-
1961		150	27	502	8	2-32	62.75	-
1962		51.3	8	228	4	2-25	57.00	-
1963		76	26	163	8	4-40	20.37	-
1964		138.4	34	365	12	5-46	30.41	1
1965		118.2	26	314	15	5-88	20.93	1
1966		92	18	282	10	3-45	28.20	-
1967		165.2	34	471	19	5-51	24.78	1
1968		260	64	707	24	5-47	29.45	1
Total		**1590.5**	**328**	**4729**	**133**	**5-46**	**35.55**	**4**

For Surrey Against Each Opponent (Batting and Fielding)

	M	I	NO	R	HS	Ave	100	50	Ct
County Championship									
Derbyshire	12	20	2	362	50	20.11	-	1	19
Essex	19	32	9	1186	130	51.56	2	8	18
Glamorgan	14	18	0	403	59	22.38	-	4	15
Gloucestershire	21	35	8	1254	124*	46.44	3	9	18
Hampshire	16	27	3	1052	151*	43.83	4	3	15
Kent	21	32	6	1120	150*	43.07	3	4	25
Lancashire	16	24	7	1277	135*	75.11	4	7	16
Leicestershire	17	25	5	592	101*	29.60	1	2	22
Middlesex	26	42	2	1273	166	31.82	3	7	28
Northamptonshire	19	27	4	905	109*	39.34	2	6	24
Nottinghamshire	27	43	11	1856	207	58.00	6	7	28
Somerset	12	19	2	480	73	28.23	-	2	17
Sussex	21	36	6	923	96*	30.76	-	7	24

Warwickshire	16	24	5	992	186	52.21	3	4	11
Worcestershire	19	29	6	910	142*	39.56	2	2	13
Yorkshire	27	44	5	1204	158*	30.87	1	10	32
Total	**303**	**477**	**81**	**15789**	**207**	**39.87**	**34**	**83**	**325**

Other Matches

Australians	5	8	1	160	68*	22.85	-	1	1
Cambridge University	13	14	4	731	149	73.10	1	5	15
Combined Services	1	2	1	117	110*	117.00	1	-	1
Indians	3	6	3	327	85	109.00	-	3	3
MCC	13	21	2	506	82	26.63	-	4	9
New Zealanders	3	4	1	228	129*	76.00	1	1	7
Oxford University	9	10	4	509	146	84.83	1	3	9
Pakistanis	2	3	0	118	102	39.33	1	-	1
Rest	3	6	0	178	136	29.66	1	-	5
Rhodesia	2	4	0	165	111	41.25	1	-	3
South Africans	1	2	0	39	34	19.50	-	-	-
West Indians	4	7	2	330	110*	66.00	2	-	3
Total	**362**	**564**	**99**	**19197**	**207**	**41.28**	**43**	**100**	**382**

For Surrey Against Each Opponent (Bowling)

	O	M	R	W	BB	Ave	5i
County Championship							
Derbyshire	47	11	116	5	4-59	23.20	-
Essex	104.4	30	317	11	2-12	28.81	-
Glamorgan	66.4	13	179	8	3-39	22.37	-
Gloucestershire	130.2	28	384	11	5-47	34.90	1
Hampshire	46	5	176	1	1-32	176.00	-
Kent	56	9	211	2	1-13	105.00	-
Lancashire	27.1	7	68	1	1-18	68.00	-
Leicestershire	32	5	98	1	1-51	98.00	-
Middlesex	81.4	19	219	4	2-5	54.75	-
Northamptonshire	72.1	15	236	6	2-18	39.33	-
Nottinghamshire	181	38	503	13	4-40	38.69	-
Somerset	47	6	131	2	1-2	65.50	-
Sussex	106	19	310	7	2-34	44.28	-
Warwickshire	71.2	19	187	6	4-57	31.16	-
Worcestershire	46	13	124	0	-	-	-
Yorkshire	157.2	30	468	18	5-51	26.00	1
Total	**1272.3**	**267**	**3727**	**96**	**5-47**	**38.82**	**2**
Other Matches							
Australians	8	1	39	0	-	-	-
Cambridge University	39.2	9	127	6	4-31	21.16	-
Combined Services	3	1	12	1	1-12	12.00	-
Indians	15	3	52	1	1-22	52.00	-
MCC	29	4	135	5	5-46	27.00	1
New Zealanders	43.4	5	115	9	5-88	12.77	1
Oxford University	113.2	27	304	10	3-27	30.40	-
Pakistanis	7	0	36	0	-	-	-
Rhodesia	46	8	131	5	3-48	26.20	-
West Indians	14	3	51	0	-	-	-
Total	**1590.5**	**328**	**4729**	**133**	**5-46**	**35.55**	**4**

For Other Teams Against Each Opponent
(Batting and Fielding)

	M	I	NO	R	HS	Ave	100	50	Ct
Commonwealth XI									
Invitation XI	1	2	0	49	41	24.50	-	-	1
Natal	1	2	0	11	7	5.50	-	-	-
Rhodesia	1	2	0	97	66	48.50	-	1	2
Transvaal	1	1	0	7	7	7.00	-	-	-
Total	**4**	**7**	**0**	**164**	**66**	**23.42**	**-**	**1**	**3**
England XI									
Commonwealth XI	1	2	0	131	75	65.50	-	2	1
Rest of World XI	2	3	1	32	13	16.00	-	-	1
Total	**3**	**5**	**1**	**163**	**75**	**40.75**	**-**	**2**	**2**
MCC in England									
Australians	1	2	0	90	55	45.00	-	1	1
Cambridge University	1	2	1	73	62*	73.00	-	1	-
South Africans	1	2	0	30	27	15.00	-	-	-
Yorkshire	2	4	0	200	107	50.00	1	1	2
Total	**5**	**10**	**1**	**393**	**107**	**43.66**	**1**	**3**	**3**
MCC Overseas									
Amir of Bahawalpur XI	1	1	0	18	18	18.00	-	-	-
Australian XI	1	2	1	238	219	238.00	1	-	1
Barbados	2	3	1	227	79	113.50	-	3	-
Berbice	1	1	0	103	103	103.00	1	-	-
Ceylon	1	2	1	95	93	95.00	-	1	1
Combined Railways and Baluchistan									
	1	1	0	41	41	41.00	-	-	2
Combined Universities	2	2	1	163	149	163.00	1	-	2
Combined XI (Australia)	4	5	0	157	73	31.40	-	1	4
Combined XI (India)	1	1	0	0	0	0.00	-	-	-
East Pakistan	1	1	0	65	65	65.00	-	1	1
East Zone	1	2	2	84	80*	-	-	1	-
Eastern Province	1	1	0	2	2	2.00	-	-	-
Governor's XI	1	2	0	55	55	27.50	-	1	1
Griqualand West	1	1	0	10	10	10.00	-	-	-
Jamaica	2	3	0	68	32	22.66	-	-	1
Karachi	1	2	2	74	70*	-	-	1	-
Leeward Island	2	2	1	183	100*	183.00	1	1	-
N.E.Transvaal	1	1	0	45	45	45.00	-	-	2
North Zone	1	-							
Orange Free State	1	2	1	37	34	37.00	-	-	2
Otago	1	1	0	18	18	18.00	-	-	-
Pakistan	4	8	0	186	52	23.25	-	1	1
Pakistan Services	1	1	0	35	35	35.00	-	-	1
President's XI (India)	3	5	1	105	76	26.25	-	1	5
President's XI (West Indies)	1	2	1	54	53*	27.00	-	1	2
Punjab C A	1	1	0	87	87	87.00	-	1	-
Queensland	2	3	3	272	183*	-	1	1	2
Rajasthan	1	1	0	91	91	91.00	-	1	1
Rhodesia	1	2	1	100	74	100.00	-	1	-
S. A. Universities	1	1	0	6	6	6.00	-	-	-
Sind C A	1	1	0	66	66	66.00	-	1	-
South Australia	4	6	1	391	104	78.20	1	5	5
South Zone	2	2	0	111	108	55.50	1	-	1
Transvaal	1	1	0	169	169	169.00	1	-	-
Trinidad	3	6	1	45	17	9.00	-	-	5
Victoria	2	4	0	269	158	67.25	1	1	1
Western Australia	1	1	0	24	24	24.00	-	-	-

Western Province	1	2	1	251	169*	251.00	1	1	-
West Zone	1	1	0	72	72	72.00	-	1	1
Windward Islands	2	2	0	33	24	16.50	-	-	1
Total	61	86	19	4050	219	60.44	10	26	43

MCC Australian Touring Team

Rest	1	2	0	24	23	12.00	-	-	-

Players

Gentlemen	7	11	0	484	111	44.00	2	3	14

Rest

Yorkshire	2	4	0	63	19	15.75	-	-	-

South

North	2	4	0	167	52	41.75	-	1	3

T.N.Pearce's XI

Indians	1	2	0	80	48	40.00	-	-	4
Pakistanis	2	3	1	77	46	38.50	-	-	1
South Africans	1	2	0	46	27	23.00	-	-	1
Total	4	7	1	203	48	33.83	-	-	6

TOTAL -Other Teams	89	136	22	5711	219	50.09	13	36	74
OVERALL TOTAL	533	831	136	31714	256	45.63	76	171	514

For Other Teams Against Each Opponent (Bowling)

	O	M	R	W	BB	Ave	5i
Commonwealth XI							
Invitation XI	23	3	87	5	4-42	17.40	-
Natal	10	1	32	0	-	-	-
Rhodesia	12	1	37	1	1-37	37.00	-
Transvaal	13	1	44	1	1-44	44.00	-
Total	58	6	200	7	4-42	28.57	-
England XI							
Rest of World XI	9.4	0	66	2	1-14	33.00	-
MCC in England							
Australians	10	1	49	1	1-28	49.00	-
Yorkshire	7	2	11	1	1-11	11.00	-
Total	17	3	60	2	1-11	30.00	-
MCC Overseas							
Amir of Bahawalpur XI	1	0	3	1	1-3	3.00	-
Barbados	35	6	108	1	1-58	108.00	-
Berbice	5	0	18	0	-	-	-
Combined Universities	25.1	9	42	3	2-3	14.00	-
Combined XI (Australia)	20.4	1	109	2	1-8	54.50	-
East Zone	21	6	63	2	2-63	31.50	-
Eastern Province	4.1	1	17	3	3-17	5.66	-
Governor's XI	9	2	24	0	-	-	-
Griqualand West	30.5	10	69	9	7-40	7.66	1
Jamaica	35.5	8	132	4	2-34	33.00	-
Karachi	10	1	38	0	-	-	-
Leeward Islands	55.3	10	158	1	1-56	158.00	-
N.E.Transvaal	1	0	1	0	-	-	-
North Zone	10	1	31	3	2-18	10.33	-
Otago	10	2	41	3	3-41	13.66	-

Pakistan Services	1	1	0	0	-	-	-
President's XI (India)	21	3	69	2	2-53	34.50	-
President's XI (West Indies)	31	4	129	5	5-99	25.80	1
Queensland	20	4	99	1	1-71	99.00	-
S. A. Universities	30	11	54	9	5-29	6.00	1
South Australia	26	2	109	3	3-55	36.33	-
South Zone	19.2	6	56	5	3-11	11.20	-
Trinidad	75.1	11	224	7	3-42	32.00	-
Victoria	30.6	4	107	7	4-24	15.28	-
Western Australia	10	1	47	0	-	-	-
West Zone	6.3	1	30	2	1-1	15.00	-
Windward Islands	7.2	3	12	2	2-6	6.00	-
Total (6-ball)	**444.5**	**96** }	**1790**	**75**	**7-40**	**23.86**	**3**
(8-ball)	**107.2**	**12** }					

MCC Australian Touring Team

Rest	**1**	**0**	**4**	**1**	**1-4**	**4.00**	-

Players

Gentlemen	**62**	**8**	**275**	**8**	**4-59**	**34.37**	-

Rest

Yorkshire	**32**	**5**	**105**	**5**	**3-18**	**21.00**	-

South

North	**31.4**	**3**	**161**	**7**	**6-70**	**23.00**	**1**

T.N.Pearce's XI

Indians	4	0	15	0	-	-	-
Pakistanis	8	0	41	0	-	-	-
South Africans	29	1	161	4	2-67	40.25	-
Total	**41**	**1**	**217**	**4**	**2-67**	**54.25**	-

TOTAL - Other Teams	**697.2**	**135** }	**2878**	**111**	**7-40**	**25.92**	**4**
(8-ball)	**107.2**	**12** }					
OVERALL TOTAL	**2678.3**	**564** }	**8907**	**273**	**7-40**	**32.62**	**8**
(8-ball)	**153.6**	**18** }					

Record on Each Ground (Batting and Fielding)

	M	I	NO	R	HS	Ave	100	50	Ct
In England									
Surrey Grounds									
Guildford	15	22	7	1040	149	69.33	3	5	20
Kennington Oval	186	287	51	9867	207	41.80	20	53	204
Other English Grounds									
Ashby-de-la-Zouch	1	2	0	6	5	3.00	-	-	-
Basingstoke	1	2	0	30	22	15.00	-	-	1
Blackheath	9	13	2	419	121	38.09	1	2	13
Bournemouth	1	2	0	31	19	15.50	-	-	-
Bradford	5	8	0	197	76	24.62	-	2	9
Bramall Lane	5	10	2	291	79*	36.37	-	2	2
Bristol	4	6	0	86	56	14.33	-	1	4
Cardiff	3	5	0	91	59	18.20	-	1	4
Cheltenham	4	8	1	236	103	33.71	1	1	2
Chesterfield	2	1	0	3	3	3.00	-	-	2
Clacton-on-Sea	3	5	1	169	129*	42.25	1	-	4
Colchester	1	2	1	34	32*	17.00	-	-	1
Coventry	1	2	0	83	49	41.50	-	-	-
Derby	2	4	2	38	27*	19.00	-	-	4
Eastbourne	1	2	0	77	50	38.50	-	1	1

Edgbaston	13	21	3	917	186	50.94	4	2	10
Fenner's	8	8	1	415	97	59.28	-	4	8
Gloucester	3	5	1	219	89	54.75	-	2	3
Gravesend	1	1	1	150	150*	-	1	-	-
Hastings	1	2	0	113	95	56.50	-	1	1
Headingley	10	16	2	726	163	51.85	1	4	11
Hove	7	13	4	318	96	35.33	-	3	9
Hull	1	2	0	19	10	9.50	-	-	1
Ilford	1	2	0	62	39	31.00	-	-	-
Kettering	1	2	0	39	22	19.50	-	-	1
Leicester	5	7	1	183	101*	30.50	1	-	2
Leyton	2	4	1	112	62*	37.33	-	1	2
Lord's	47	76	4	2259	166	31.37	2	18	44
Neath	1	2	0	41	24	20.50	-	-	-
Northampton	8	10	2	471	109	58.87	1	4	7
Nuneaton	1	-							
Old Trafford	15	25	6	1475	256	77.63	4	7	14
The Parks	3	2	0	56	30	28.00	-	-	2
Portsmouth	3	5	0	218	100	43.60	1	1	5
Romford	1	2	1	47	41	47.00	-	-	1
Scarborough	12	21	2	914	136	48.10	4	2	14
Southampton	3	5	1	293	100*	73.25	1	1	-
Southport	1	2	0	80	68	40.00	-	1	1
Stroud	1	2	1	112	61*	112.00	-	2	-
Swansea	2	2	0	69	59	34.50	-	1	-
Taunton	2	3	0	15	8	5.00	-	-	4
Torquay	3	6	0	298	75	49.66	-	3	4
Trent Bridge	18	29	9	1132	126	56.60	5	4	19
Weston-super-Mare	3	5	1	101	40*	25.25	-	-	4
Worcester	9	15	1	324	99	23.14	-	1	3
Total - In England	**430**	**676**	**109**	**23876**	**256**	**42.10**	**51**	**130**	**441**

In Australia

Adelaide	6	10	2	748	132*	93.50	3	7	7
Brisbane	4	7	3	464	183*	116.00	1	3	4
Hobart	1	1	0	37	37	37.00	-	-	2
Launceston	1	1	0	73	73	73.00	-	1	1
Melbourne	6	11	3	752	219*	94.00	3	2	6
Perth	3	4	0	71	44	17.75	-	-	1
Sydney	3	5	0	252	101	50.40	1	1	1
Total	**24**	**39**	**8**	**2397**	**219***	**77.32**	**8**	**14**	**22**

In India

Ahmedabad	1	1	0	72	72	72.00	-	1	1
Bangalore	2	2	1	79	76	79.00	-	1	-
Bombay	1	2	2	203	151*	-	1	1	1
Calcutta	1	2	0	17	14	8.50	-	-	1
Cuttack	1	2	2	84	80*	-	-	1	-
Delhi	1	1	1	113	113*	-	1	-	-
Hyderabad	2	3	0	122	108	40.66	1	-	4
Jaipur	1	1	0	91	91	91.00	-	1	1
Jullundur	1	-							-
Kanpur	1	2	0	193	172	96.50	1	-	-
Madras (Nehru Stadium)	2	3	0	148	80	49.33	-	1	-
Poona	1	1	1	149	149*	-	1	-	1
Total	**15**	**20**	**7**	**1271**	**151***	**97.76**	**5**	**6**	**9**

In New Zealand

Auckland	1	1	0	126	126	126.00	1	-	1
Christchurch	1	2	0	92	47	46.00	-	-	1
Dunedin	1	1	0	18	18	18.00	-	-	-
Wellington	1	1	0	76	76	76.00	-	1	3
Total	**4**	**5**	**0**	**312**	**126**	**62.40**	**1**	**1**	**5**

In South Africa

Bloemfontein	1	2	1	37	34*	37.00	-	-	2
Bulawayo	1	2	0	24	20	12.00	-	-	3
Cape Town	2	4	2	314	169*	157.00	1	1	-
Durban	2	3	1	159	148*	79.50	1	-	1
Johannesburg	5	7	0	450	169	64.28	2	1	1
Kimberley (De Beers Stadium)	1	1	0	10	10	10.00	-	-	-
Pietermaritzburg	1	1	0	6	6	6.00	-	-	-
Port Elizabeth	2	2	0	74	72	37.00	-	1	2
Pretoria	1	1	0	45	45	45.00	-	-	2
Salisbury	3	6	1	338	111	67.60	1	2	2
Total	**19**	**29**	**5**	**1457**	**169***	**60.70**	**5**	**5**	**13**

In Ceylon

Colombo	1	2	1	95	93	95.00	-	1	1

In Pakistan

Bahawalpur	2	2	0	18	18	9.00	-	-	-
Chittagong	1	1	0	65	65	65.00	-	1	1
Dacca	2	3	0	138	84	45.46	-	1	1
Hyderabad	1	1	0	66	66	66.00	-	1	-
Karachi	2	4	2	112	70*	56.00	-	1	1
Lahore	3	5	0	221	139	44.20	1	1	1
Lyallpur	2	3	0	142	87	47.33	-	2	1
Muljan	1	1	0	41	41	41.00	-	-	2
Peshawar	1	2	0	32	32	16.00	-	-	-
Rawalpindi	1	2	0	15	11	7.50	-	-	2
Sargodha	1	1	0	35	35	35.00	-	-	1
Total	**17**	**25**	**2**	**885**	**139**	**38.47**	**1**	**7**	**10**

In West Indies

Antigua	2	2	1	183	100*	183.00	1	1	-
Bridgetown	5	7	2	426	128	85.20	1	4	3
Castries	1	1	0	24	24	24.00	-	-	-
Georgetown	2	4	0	31	27	7.75	-	-	-
Grenada	1	1	0	9	9	9.00	-	-	1
Kingston (Melbourne Park)	1	1	0	30	30	30.00	-	-	1
Kingston (Sabina Park)	3	6	0	134	63	22.33	-	1	-
Point-a-Pierre	1	2	1	10	8	10.00	-	-	1
Port of Spain	6	10	0	471	143	47.10	2	1	7
Rose Hall	1	1	0	103	103	103.00	1	-	-
Total	**23**	**35**	**4**	**1421**	**143**	**45.83**	**5**	**7**	**13**

Total - Overseas	**103**	**155**	**27**	**7838**	**219***	**61.23**	**25**	**41**	**73**
Overall Total	**533**	**831**	**136**	**31714**	**256**	**45.63**	**76**	**171**	**514**

Record on Each Ground (Bowling)

	O	M	R	W	BB	Ave	5i
In England							
Surrey Grounds							
Guildford	80.2	15	282	2	1-14	141.00	-
Kennington Oval	965.4	201	2709	86	5-51	31.50	2
Other English Grounds							
Basingstoke	5	1	18	0	-	-	-
Blackheath	24	3	111	0	-	-	-
Bradford	8.4	0	26	1	1-26	26.00	-
Bramall Lane	6	0	32	0	-	-	-
Bristol	4	0	25	0	-	-	-

Cheltenham	19.2	5	51	5	5-47	10.20	1
Eastbourne	25	4	73	2	2-34	36.50	-
Edgbaston	55	14	153	4	4-57	38.25	-
Fenner's	22.2	5	82	6	4-31	13.66	-
Headingley	36	8	121	3	2-232	40.33	-
Hove	34	2	147	2	1-18	73.50	-
Leicester	2	0	5	0	-	-	-
Lord's	127.4	20	469	15	5-46	31.26	1
Neath	10.4	2	35	2	2-20	17.50	-
Northampton	21.2	5	84	1	1-28	84.00	-
Old Trafford	58.1	12	154	6	3-36	25.66	-
The Parks	43	12	97	5	3-27	19.40	-
Romford	5.4	3	6	1	1-6	6.00	-
Scarborough	109.4	12	507	13	4-59	39.00	-
Southampton	12	2	48	0	-	-	-
Stroud	5	2	8	0	-	-	-
Taunton	15	2	49	0	-	-	-
Torquay	20.4	0	112	7	6-70	16.00	1
Trent Bridge	86	14	292	4	3-45	73.00	-
Weston-super-Mare	2	0	2	1	1-2	2.00	-
Worcester	46	13	124	0	-	-	-
Total - In England	**1850.1**	**357**	**5822**	**166**	**6-70**	**35.07**	**5**
In Australia							
Adelaide	26	2	109	3	3-55	36.33	-
Brisbane	32	7	143	2	1-44	71.50	-
Hobart	10	0	42	0	-	-	-
Launceston	4.4	1	24	2	1-8	12.00	-
Melbourne	49.2	4	199	9	4-24	22.11	-
Perth	16	1	90	0	-	-	-
Sydney	16	3	65	0	-	-	-
Total	**153.6**	**18**	**672**	**16**	**4-24**	**42.00**	**-**
In India							
Ahmedabad	6.3	1	30	2	1-1	15.00	-
Bangalore	8	2	16	0	-	-	-
Bombay	3	0	18	0	-	-	-
Cuttack	21	6	63	2	2-63	31.50	-
Delhi	9	1	39	0	-	-	-
Hyderabad	32.2	7	109	7	3-11	15.57	-
Jullundur	10	1	31	3	2-18	10.33	-
Madras (Nehru Stadium)	6	0	29	0	-	-	-
Poona	9	2	14	2	2-3	7.00	-
Total	**104.5**	**20**	**349**	**16**	**3-11**	**21.81**	**-**
In New Zealand							
Auckland	12	4	38	0	-	-	-
Christchurch	5	0	18	0	-	-	-
Dunedin	10	2	41	3	3-41	13.66	-
Wellington	13.3	4	33	4	3-32	8.25	-
Total	**40.3**	**10**	**130**	**7**	**3-32**	**18.57**	**-**
In South Africa							
Bulawayo	23	3	83	2	2-83	41.50	-
Capetown	3.1	1	4	3	3-4	1.33	-
Durban	10	1	32	0	-	-	-
Johannesburg	40	4	160	6	4-42	26.66	-
Kimberley (De Beers Stadium)	30.5	10	69	9	7-40	7.66	1
Pietermaritzburg	30	11	54	9	5-29	6.00	1
Port Elizabeth	4.1	1	17	3	3-17	5.66	-
Pretoria	1	0	1	0	-	-	-
Salisbury	35	6	85	4	3-48	21.25	-
Total	**177.1**	**37**	**505**	**36**	**7-40**	**14.02**	**2**

In Pakistan

	Overs	Mdns	Runs	Wkts	Best	Avge	5wi
Bahawalpur	1	0	3	1	1-3	3.00	-
Dacca	32	14	56	0	-	-	-
Karachi	10	1	38	0	-	-	-
Lahore	22.1	7	53	1	1-8	53.00	-
Lyallpur	9	2	24	0	-	-	-
Sargodha	1	1	0	0	-	-	-
Total	**75.1**	**25**	**174**	**2**	**1-3**	**87.00**	**-**

In West Indies

	Overs	Mdns	Runs	Wkts	Best	Avge	5wi
Antigua	55.3	10	158	1	1-56	158.00	-
Bridgetown	96	14	343	8	5-99	42.87	1
Castries	2	0	6	0	-	-	-
Georgetown	24	6	65	1	1-43	65.00	-
Grenada	5.2	3	6	2	2-6	3.00	-
Kingston (Melbourne Park)	23.5	4	92	2	2-44	46.00	-
Kingston (Sabina Park)	43	16	92	3	2-34	30.66	-
Point-a-Pierre	29.5	5	105	4	3-42	26.25	-
Port of Spain	146.1	39	370	9	2-23	41.11	-
Rose Hall	5	0	18	0	-	-	-
Total	**430.4**	**97**	**1255**	**30**	**5-99**	**41.83**	**1**

	Overs	Mdns	Runs	Wkts	Best	Avge	5wi
Total - Overseas (6-ball)	**828.2**	**189 ⎱ 18 ⎰**	**3085**	**107**	**7-40**	**28.83**	**3**
(8-ball)	153.6						
Overall Total (6-ball)	**2678.3**	**546 ⎱ 18 ⎰**	**8907**	**273**	**7-40**	**32.62**	**8**
(8-ball)	153.6						

Centuries in First-Class Cricket (76)

For England (20)

256	v Australia	Old Trafford	1964
132*	v Australia	Adelaide	1962/63
115	v Australia	Melbourne	1965/66
102	v Australia	Adelaide	1965/66
101	v Australia	Sydney	1962/63
172	v India	Kanpur	1961/62
151*	v India	Bombay	1961/62
113*	v India	Delhi	1961/62
163	v New Zealand	Headingley	1965
137	v New Zealand	Edgbaston	1965
126	v New Zealand	Auckland	1962/63
148	v Pakistan	Lord's	1967
142	v Pakistan	Kennington Oval	1967
139	v Pakistan	Lahore	1961/62
109*	v Pakistan	Trent Bridge	1967
148*	v South Africa	Durban	1964/65
121	v South Africa	Johannesburg	1964/65
143	v West Indies	Port of Spain	1967/68
128	v West Indies	Bridgetown	1959/60
121	v West Indies	Port of Spain	1959/60

For Surrey (43)

130*	v Essex	Kennington Oval	1962
129*	v Essex	Clacton-on-Sea	1957
124*	v Gloucestershire	Kennington Oval	1957
108*	v Gloucestershire	Kennington Oval	1954
103	v Gloucestershire	Cheltenham	1954
151*	v Hampshire	Kennington Oval	1961
103	v Hampshire	Guildford	1956
100*	v Hampshire	Southampton	1963
100	v Hampshire	Portsmouth	1959
150*	v Kent	Gravesend	1964

126	v Kent	Kennington Oval	1960
121	v Kent	Blackheath	1961
135*	v Lancashire	Kennington Oval	1955
125*	v Lancashire	Old Trafford	1961
117*	v Lancashire	Old Trafford	1966
101	v Lancashire	Old Trafford	1962
101*	v Leicestershire	Leicester	1958
166	v Middlesex	Lord's	1959
113	v Middlesex	Kennington Oval	1967
109	v Middlesex	Kennington Oval	1965
109*	v Northamptonshire	Northampton	1956
103*	v Northamptonshire	Kennington Oval	1966
207	v Nottinghamshire	Kennington Oval	1964
163	v Nottinghamshire	Kennington Oval	1961
126	v Nottinghamshire	Trent Bridge	1955
113*	v Nottinghamshire	Trent Bridge	1959
106	v Nottinghamshire	Trent Bridge	1966
102*	v Nottinghamshire	Trent Bridge	1962
186	v Warwickshire	Edgbaston	1959
118*	v Warwickshire	Edgbaston	1959
101	v Warwickshire	Edgbaston	1957
142*	v Worcestershire	Kennington Oval	1967
136*	v Worcestershire	Kennington Oval	1964
158*	v Yorkshire	Kennington Oval	1967
149	v Cambridge University	Guildford	1959
110*	v Combined Services	Kennington Oval	1957
129*	v New Zealanders	Kennington Oval	1965
146	v Oxford University	Guildford	1962
102	v Pakistanis	Kennington Oval	1954
136	v Rest of England	Scarborough	1957
111	v Rhodesia	Salisbury	1959/60
110*	v West Indians	Kennington Oval	1963
103*	v West Indians	Kennington Oval	1957

For Players (2)

111	v Gentlemen	Scarborough	1960
100	v Gentlemen	Scarborough	1962

For MCC in England (1)

107	v Yorkshire	Scarborough	1962

For MCC Overseas (10)

219*	v Australian XI	Melbourne	1962/63
103	v Berbice	Berbice	1959/60
149*	v Combined Universities	Poona	1961/62
100*	v Leeward Islands	Antigua	1967/68
183*	v Queensland	Brisbane	1962/63
104	v South Australia	Adelaide	1962/63
108	v South Zone (India)	Hyderabad	1963/64
169	v Transvaal	Johannesburg	1964/65
158	v Victoria	Melbourne	1965/66
169	v Western Province	Cape Town	1964/65

Dismissed By

In his first-class career, Barrington was dismissed 695 times, the breakdown being:-

Bowled	163	23.5%
Leg before wicket	90	12.9%
Caught	380	54.7%
Caught and Bowled	22	3.2%
Stumped	19	2.7%
Run Out	21	3.0%

The most successful bowlers to take his wicket were:-

13 Times:	F.J.Titmus
11 Times:	R.Illingworth
10 Times:	F.S.Trueman
9 Times:	L.R.Gibbs, G.D.McKenzie
8 Times:	J.B.Mortimore, G.St.A.Sobers
7 Times:	T.L.Goddard, A.E.Moss, D.Shackleton, N.I.Thomson
6 Times:	A.K.Davidson, C.Forbes, C.C.Griffith, N.J.N.Hawke, D.R.Smith
5 Times:	W.E.Alley, T.E.Bailey, J.D.Bannister, A.Brown (Kent), L.J.Coldwell, C.D.Drybrough, C.Gladwin, W.W.Hall, A.Hurd, R.A.Hutton, B.A.Langford, R.G.Marlar, R.G.Nadkarni, P.M.Pollock, J.S.Savage, D.J.Shepherd, C.T.Spencer, J.J.Warr, D.Wilson

Hundred Partnerships in First-Class Cricket

Match No

Second Wicket (28)

118	M.J.Stewart	Surrey	v Pakistanis	Kennington Oval	1954	16
235*	M.J.Stewart	Surrey	v Combined Services	Kennington Oval	1957	109
161	M.J.Stewart	Surrey	v Cambridge University	Fenner's	1959	176
159	M.J.Stewart	Surrey	v Warwickshire	Edgbaston	1959	178
221	J.H.Edrich	Surrey	v Nottinghamshire	Trent Bridge	1959	180
127	M.J.Stewart	Surrey	v Somerset	Kennington Oval	1959	182
150	J.H.Edrich	Surrey	v Yorkshire	Kennington Oval	1959	185
171	J.H.Edrich	Surrey	v Cambridge University	Guildford	1959	187
130	P.E.Richardson	Players	v Gentlemen	Scarborough	1959	205
103	G.Pullar	ENGLAND	v WEST INDIES	Bridgetown	1959/60	212
104	R.B.Simpson	Commonwealth XI	v Rhodesia	Salisbury	1960/61	253
105	J.H.Edrich	Surrey	v Hampshire	Kennington Oval	1961	258
135	J.H.Edrich	Surrey	v Northamptonshire	Northampton	1961	264
232	J.H.Edrich	Surrey	v Kent	Blackheath	1961	269
135	J.H.Edrich	Surrey	v Middlesex	Lord's	1961	279
139	G.Pullar	ENGLAND	v INDIA	Kanpur	1961/62	288
164	G.Pullar	ENGLAND	v INDIA	Delhi	1961/62	290
147	G.Pullar	ENGLAND	v PAKISTAN	Dacca	1961/62	295
316*	M.J.Stewart	Surrey	v Essex	Kennington Oval	1962	305
122	P.B.H.May	Surrey	v Sussex	Kennington Oval	1962	310
204*	P.B.H.May	Surrey	v Middlesex	Kennington Oval	1962	315
147*	M.J.Stewart	Surrey	v Essex	Leyton	1962	321
107	J.H.Edrich	Surrey	v Derbyshire	Kennington Oval	1963	346
202	M.J.Stewart	Surrey	v Essex	Kennington Oval	1963	349
130	M.J.Stewart	MCC	v President's XI	Bangalore	1963/64	372
163	R.A.E.Tindall	Surrey	v Gloucestershire	Gloucester	1964	387
369	J.H.Edrich	ENGLAND	v NEW ZEALAND	Headingley	1965	427
129	G.Boycott	ENGLAND	v INDIA	Headingley	1967	480

Third Wicket (53)

104	W.E.Jones	South	v North	Torquay	1955	62
126	P.E.Richardson	MCC	v Sind C A	Hyderabad	1955/56	65
101	M.Tompkin	MCC	v Pakistan	Lahore	1955/56	68
142	M.J.Stewart	Surrey	v Hampshire	Guildford	1956	87
157	B.Constable	Surrey	v Sussex	Hastings	1956	94
168	B.Constable	Surrey	v Gloucestershire	Kennington Oval	1957	120
112	M.J.Stewart	Surrey	v Gloucestershire	Bristol	1957	130
184	M.J.Stewart	Surrey	v Warwickshire	Edgbaston	1957	137
117	B.Constable	Surrey	v Essex	Clacton-on-Sea	1957	138
150	D.B.Close	An England XI	v A Commonwealth XI	Torquay	1958	175
169	B.Constable	Surrey	v Indians	Kennington Oval	1959	179
206	T.H.Clark	Surrey	v Middlesex	Lord's	1959	198
150	T.H.Clark	Surrey	v Hampshire	Portsmouth	1959	200
168	E.R.Dexter	MCC	v Leeward Islands	Antigua	1959/60	218
283	J.M.Parks	MCC	v Berbice	Blairmont	1959/60	220

147	A.B.D.Parsons	Surrey	v Lancashire	Old Trafford	1960	226
249	M.J.Stewart	Surrey	v Kent	Kennington Oval	1960	232
136	D.G.W.Fletcher	Surrey	v Yorkshire	Bramall Lane	1960	240
134	J.H.Edrich	Surrey	v Middlesex	Lord's	1960	246
118	B.Constable	Surrey	v Gloucestershire	Kennington Oval	1961	263
149*	B.Constable	Surrey	v Sussex	Hove	1961	266
192	M.J.K.Smith	ENGLAND	v PAKISTAN	Lahore	1961/62	283
129	P.H.Parfitt	MCC	v All Ceylon	Colombo	1961/62	297
123	B.Constable	Surrey	v Kent	Blackheath	1962	313
168	T.W.Graveney	MCC	v South Australia	Adelaide	1962/63	329
147	D.S.Sheppard	MCC	v Combined XI	Launceston	1962/63	335
116	E.R.Dexter	MCC	v Victoria	Melbourne	1962/63	338
144	M.J.Stewart	Surrey	v Yorkshire	Bradford	1964	384
246	E.R.Dexter	ENGLAND	v AUSTRALIA	Old Trafford	1964	390
137	J.M.Brearley	MCC	v Western Province	Cape Town	1964/65	401
191	E.R.Dexter	ENGLAND	v SOUTH AFRICA	Johannesburg	1964/65	405
121*	J.H.Edrich	Surrey	v Cambridge University	Fenner's	1965	411
225	J.H.Edrich	Surrey	v New Zealanders	Kennington Oval	1965	420
129	J.H.Edrich	Surrey	v Yorkshire	Bradford	1965	426
118	J.H.Edrich	ENGLAND	v AUSTRALIA	Melbourne	1965/66	445
178	J.H.Edrich	ENGLAND	v AUSTRALIA	Melbourne	1965/66	449
139	J.H.Edrich	Surrey	v Nottinghamshire	Trent Bridge	1966	456
153	R.A.E.Tindall	Surrey	v Nottinghamshire	Trent Bridge	1966	456
115	M.J.Stewart	Surrey	v Gloucestershire	Cheltenham	1966	465
134	J.H.Edrich	Surrey	v Gloucestershire	Kennington Oval	1966	467
141	M.J.Edwards	Surrey	v MCC	Lord's	1967	471
114	M.J.Stewart	Surrey	v Warwickshire	Kennington Oval	1967	472
106	J.H.Edrich	Surrey	v Hampshire	Kennington Oval	1967	473
167	M.J.Stewart	Surrey	v Northamptonshire	Northampton	1967	474
141	J.H.Edrich	Surrey	v Indians	Kennington Oval	1967	478
297	J.H.Edrich	Surrey	v Middlesex	Kennington Oval	1967	486
201	T.W.Graveney	ENGLAND	v PAKISTAN	Lord's	1967	490
141	T.W.Graveney	ENGLAND	v PAKISTAN	Kennington Oval	1967	494
134	M.C.Cowdrey	ENGLAND	v WEST INDIES	Port of Spain	1967/68	500
110	G.Boycott	MCC	v Leeward Islands	Antigua	1967/68	503
101	M.C.Cowdrey	ENGLAND	v WEST INDIES	Kingston	1967/68	502
133	M.C.Cowdrey	ENGLAND	v WEST INDIES	Port of Spain	1967/68	507
122	M.J.Stewart	Surrey	v Nottinghamshire	Trent Bridge	1968	526

Fourth Wicket (36)

128	P.B.H.May	Surrey	v Cambridge University	Fenner's	1955	29
218*	P.B.H.May	Surrey	v Lancashire	Kennington Oval	1955	35
130	P.B.H.May	Surrey	v Yorkshire	Kennington Oval	1957	123
156*	B.Constable	Surrey	v West Indians	Kennington Oval	1957	131
107	P.B.H.May	Surrey	v Hampshire	Portsmouth	1957	133
152	P.B.H.May	Surrey	v The Rest	Scarborough	1957	141
145	P.B.H.May	Surrey	v Lancashire	Old Trafford	1958	149
110	B.Constable	Surrey	v Cambridge University	Guildford	1958	155
125	P.B.H.May	ENGLAND	v INDIA	Trent Bridge	1959	184
193	M.C.Cowdrey	ENGLAND	v INDIA	Headingley	1959	189
109	M.J.K.Smith	ENGLAND	v INDIA	Old Trafford	1959	194
142	E.R.Dexter	ENGLAND	v WEST INDIES	Port of Spain	1959/60	215
161	E.R.Dexter	ENGLAND	v AUSTRALIA	Edgbaston	1961	265
161	E.R.Dexter	ENGLAND	v INDIA	Bombay	1961/62	285
206	E.R.Dexter	ENGLAND	v INDIA	Kanpur	1961/62	288
103	D.S.Sheppard	MCC	v Combined XI	Perth	1962/63	328
166	M.C.Cowdrey	ENGLAND	v NEW ZEALAND	Auckland	1962/63	340
111*	B.Constable	Surrey	v Leicestershire	Kennington Oval	1963	347
114	P.B.H.May	Surrey	v Sussex	Guildford	1963	355
116	R.A.E.Tindall	Surrey	v Yorkshire	Kennington Oval	1963	358
193*	M.D.Willett	Surrey	v Yorkshire	Bramall Lane	1963	360
192	D.Wilson	MCC	v South Zone	Hyderabad	1963/64	373
119	J.B.Bolus	ENGLAND	v INDIA	Madras	1963/64	374
230	M.D.Willett	Surrey	v Kent	Gravesend	1964	379

153*	M.D.Willett	Surrey	v Worcestershire	Kennington Oval	1964	381
110	M.D.Willett	Surrey	v Essex	Kennington Oval	1964	382
108	M.D.Willett	Surrey	v Lancashire	Southport	1964	388
146	P.H.Parfitt	MCC	v Rhodesia	Salisbury	1964/65	398
100	P.H.Parfitt	ENGLAND	v SOUTH AFRICA	Johannesburg	1964/65	408
157	G.Boycott	ENGLAND	v SOUTH AFRICA	Port Elizabeth	1964/65	410
136	M.C.Cowdrey	ENGLAND	v NEW ZEALAND	Edgbaston	1965	418
135	M.C.Cowdrey	ENGLAND	v SOUTH AFRICA	Kennington Oval	1965	436
160	M.C.Cowdrey	MCC	v Victoria	Melbourne	1965/66	441
188	T.W.Graveney	ENGLAND	v WEST INDIES	Port of Spain	1967/68	500
126	Younis Ahmed	Surrey	v Northamptonshire	Northampton	1968	530

Fifth Wicket (13)

117	D.G.W.Fletcher	Surrey	v Gloucestershire	Kennington Oval	1954	15
142	R.Subba Row	Surrey	v Gloucestershire	Cheltenham	1954	24
177	A.J.W.McIntyre	Surrey	v Nottinghamshire	Trent Bridge	1955	36
114	E.A.Bedser	Surrey	v Middlesex	Lord's	1955	58
103	R.Swetman	Surrey	v Cambridge University	Fenner's	1960	222
172	R.Subba Row	ENGLAND	v AUSTRALIA	Kennington Oval	1961	280
133	J.T.Murray	MCC	v Combined Universities	Poona	1961/62	284
101*	T.W.Graveney	ENGLAND	v AUSTRALIA	Adelaide	1962/63	337
106	R.A.E.Tindall	Surrey	v Nottinghamshire	Kennington Oval	1963	363
143	J.M.Parks	ENGLAND	v AUSTRALIA	Old Trafford	1964	390
114	M.D.Willett	Surrey	v Nottinghamshire	Kennington Oval	1964	391
232	M.J.K.Smith	MCC	v Transvaal	Johannesburg	1964/65	399
136	M.J.K.Smith	MCC	v South Australia	Adelaide	1965/66	444

Sixth Wicket (9)

103	A.F.Brazier	Surrey	v Worcestershire	Kennington Oval	1953	7
108	B.R.Knight	MCC	v Rajasthan	Jaipur	1961/62	287
209	B.R.Knight	MCC	v Australian XI	Melbourne	1962/63	330
180	B.R.Knight	MCC	v Queensland	Brisbane	1962/63	331
126*	M.C.Cowdrey	ENGLAND	v AUSTRALIA	Kennington Oval	1964	394
206*	J.M.Parks	ENGLAND	v SOUTH AFRICA	Durban	1964/65	402
101	S.J.Storey	Surrey	v Middlesex	Kennington Oval	1965	428
106*	F.J.Titmus	MCC	v Queensland	Brisbane	1965/66	442
140*	G.R.J.Roope	Surrey	v Worcestershire	Kennington Oval	1967	481

Seventh Wicket (2)

154	A.J.W.McIntyre	Surrey	v Leicestershire	Leicester	1958	166
122	D.J.S.Taylor	Surrey	v Yorkshire	Kennington Oval	1967	489

Eigthth Wicket (1)

198	J.C.Laker	Surrey	v Gloucestershire	Kennington Oval	1954	15

Five Wickets in an Innings (8)

15.4	0	70	6	South	v North	Torquay	1955
14	3	46	5	Surrey	v MCC	Lord's	1964
10	2	29	5	MCC	v South African Universities	Pietermaritzburg	1964/65
12.5	5	40	7	MCC	v Griqualand West	Kimberley	1964/65
29	2	88	5	Surrey	v New Zealanders	Kennington Oval	1965
20.2	5	51	5	Surrey	v Yorkshire	Kennington Oval	1967
27	4	99	5	MCC	v President's XI	Bridgetown	1967/68
17.2	4	47	5	Surrey	v Gloucestershire	Cheltenham	1968

Batsmen Dismissed

During his Career, Barrington took 273 wickets but the most dismissals of any one batsman was three being:-

K.V.Andrew, K.R.W.Fletcher, J.M.Parks, P.J.Sharpe, G.St.A.Sobers and K.Taylor

Results of Matches played

The results of the 533 first-class matches in which Barrington played were:-

	Won		Drawn		Lost	Total
Test matches	31	37.8%	39	47.6%	12 14.6%	82
Championship Matches	129	42.6%	124	40.9%	50 16.5%	303
Surrey - Other Matches	21	35.6%	25	42.4%	13 22.0%	59
Players v Gentleman	5	71.4%	2	28.6%		7
Other First-Class Matches	34	41.5%	34	41.5%	14 17.0%	82
Total	**220**	**41.3%**	**224**	**42.0%**	**89 16.7%**	**533**

Number of Catches

In the Who's Who of Cricketers by Philip Bailey, Philip Thorn and Peter Wynne-Thomas published by Hamlyn in association with the A.C.S., the number of catches made by Barrington in his career is listed as 515, which was based on a Surrey total of 383. Since publication, it has been established the Surrey figure should be 382 and, therefore, the total first-class figure is adjusted to 514 which is the figure shown in this book.

Barrington in One Day Matches

Barrington played in the early seasons of the "Gillette Cup" which started in 1963. Surrey reached the Final in 1965 when they were soundly beaten by Yorkshire.

1963

	Own Team Total	O	M	R	W	Opp Total	Ct
1. Surrey v Worcestershire, Worcester, May 22 (Worcestershire won by 114 runs)							
lbw b M.J.Horton	2 115	5	0	24	0	229-9	

SEASON'S AVERAGES

Batting and Fielding	M	I	NO	Runs	HS	Ave	100	50	Ct
Season	1	1	0	2	2	2.00	-	-	-

Bowling	O	M	R	W	BB	Ave
Season	5	0	24	0	-	-

1964

	Own Team Total	O	M	R	W	Opp Total	Ct
2. Surrey v Cheshire, Hoylake, May 6 (Surrey won by 62 runs)							
c K.F.Holding b A.L.Shillinglan	24 171-8					109	
3. Surrey v Gloucestershire, Kennington Oval, May 27 (Surrey won by 46 runs)							
c D.A.Allen b D.R.Smith	49 268-6					222	
4. Surrey v Middlesex, Kennington Oval, June 24 (Surrey won by 144 runs)							
lbw b E.A.Clark	39 236-8					122	

5. Surrey v Sussex, Hove, June 29 (Sussex won by 90 runs)
c E.R.Dexter b D.L.Bates   5   125   215-8   1

SEASON'S AVERAGES

Batting and Fielding	M	I	NO	Runs	HS	Ave	100	50	Ct
Season	4	4	0	117	49	29.25	-	-	1
Career	5	5	0	119	49	23.80	-	-	1

1965

	Own Team Total	O	M	R	W		Opp Total	Ct

6. Surrey v Glamorgan, Kennington Oval, May 22 (Surrey won by five wickets)
c J.S.Pressdee b D.J.Shepherd 1   147-5   146

7. Surrey v Northamptonshire, Kennington Oval, June 23 (Surrey won by 125 runs)
b B.S.Crump   25   222-8   97

8. Surrey v Middlesex, Kennington Oval, July 14 (Surrey won by five wickets)
not out   68   252-5   6   0   41   3   J.M.Brearley
c D.A.D.Sydenham   250-8   1
F.J.Titmus c M.J.Stewart
R.W.Hooker c S.J.Storey

9. Surrey v Yorkshire, Lord's, September 4 (Yorkshire won by 175 runs)
c J.G.Binks b F.S.Trueman   0   142   5   0   54   1   G.Boycott c S.J.Storey   317-4   1

SEASON'S AVERAGES

Batting and Fielding	M	I	NO	Runs	HS	Ave	100	50	Ct
Season	4	4	1	94	68*	31.33	-	1	2
Career	9	9	1	213	68*	26.63	-	1	3

Bowling	O	M	R	W	BB	Ave
Season	11	0	95	4	3-41	23.75
Career	16	0	119	4	3-41	29.75

1966

	Own Team Total	O	M	R	W		Opp Total	Ct

10. Surrey v Leicestershire, Leicester, May 21 (Surrey won by 46 runs)
c P.T.Marner b J.Cotton   61   231-8   2   0   13   0   185-9   1

11. Surrey v Hampshire, Bournemouth, June 22 (Hampshire won by seven wickets)
b D.W.White   46   173   174-3

SEASON'S AVERAGES

Batting and Fielding	M	I	NO	Runs	HS	Ave	100	50	Ct
Season	2	2	0	107	61	53.50	-	1	1
Career	11	11	1	320	68*	32.00	-	2	4

Bowling	O	M	R	W	BB	Ave
Season	2	0	13	0	-	-
Career	18	0	132	4	3-41	33.00

1967

	Own Team Total	O	M	R	W		Opp Total	Ct

12. Surrey v Derbyshire, Kennington Oval, May 13 (Surrey won by 184 runs)
not out   70   263-4   79

13. Surrey v Kent, Kennington Oval, June 14 (Kent won by six wickets)
    c S.E.Leary b A.L.Dixon   8   74   75-4   1

SEASON'S AVERAGES

Batting and Fielding	M	I	NO	Runs	HS	Ave	100	50	Ct
Season	2	2	1	78	70*	78.00	-	1	1
Career	13	13	2	398	70*	36.18	-	3	5

1968

	Own Team Total	O	M	R	W		Opp Total	Ct

14. Surrey v Middlesex, Lord's, May 25, 27 (Middlesex won by 103 runs)
    c R.W.Hooker b R.S.Herman   1   117   220-8

SEASON'S AVERAGES

Batting and Fielding	M	I	NO	Runs	HS	Ave	100	50	Ct
Season	1	1	0	1	1	1.00	-	-	-
Career	14	14	2	399	70	33.25	-	3	5